HARCOURT
BRACE

PHONICS
Practice Book

Grade 1

HARCOURT BRACE & COMPANY

Orlando Atlanta Austin Boston San Francisco Chicago Dallas New York
Toronto London

ISBN 0-15-309025-1

6 7 8 9 10 073 2000 99 98

CONTENTS

Harcourt Brace School Publishers

Unit 3: Short Vowels

Unit 4: Long Vowels

Harcourt Brace School Publishers

Unit 5: Consonant Clusters

Unit 6: Digraphs

Unit 7: *R-controlled Vowel: /är/ar*

Unit 8: Contractions and Possessives

Unit 9: Inflected Endings

Cut-Out Fold-Up Books

Harcourt Brace School Publishers

Phonics Practice Book

Name _____

Say the name of each picture. Color the pictures whose names begin with the same sound as .

Name _____

sun

Say the name of each picture. If it begins with the same sound as **sun**, write **S s** on the lines.

Harcourt Brace School Publishers

Help the  go over the 🏔. Color the pictures whose names begin with the same sound as 🐭 and 🏔.

Name _____

Say the name of each picture. If it begins with the same sound as **mouse**, write **Mm** on the lines.

<u>m</u>ouse

Initial Consonant: / m / m

Phonics Practice Book

Harcourt Brace School Publishers

Name _____

Say the name of each picture. Color the pictures whose names begin with the same sound as .

Name _____

fence

Say the name of each picture. If it begins with the same sound as **fence**, write **Ff** on the lines.

Initial Consonant: / f / f

Phonics Practice Book

Say the name of each picture. Color the pictures whose names begin with the same sound as 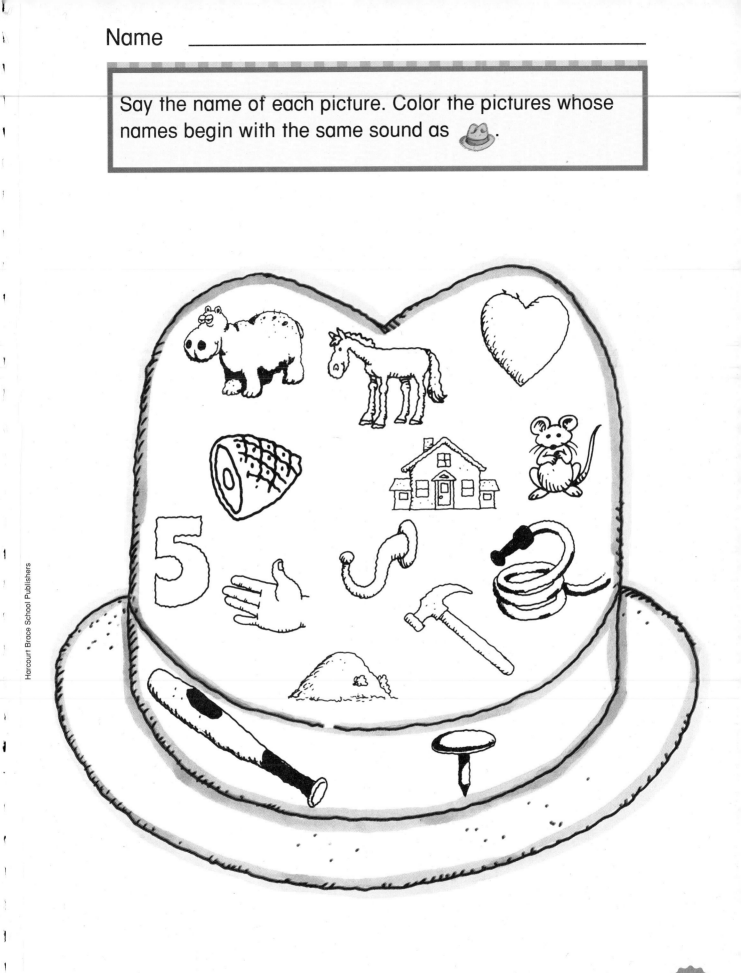.

Name _____

hat

Say the name of each picture. If it begins with the same sound as **hat**, write **Hh** on the lines.

Harcourt Brace School Publishers

Name _____

Name _____

goose

Say the name of each picture. If it begins with the same sound as **g̲oose**, write **Gg** on the lines.

1

2

3

4

5

6

7

8

9

10

11

12

Name _____

Say the name of each picture. Circle its beginning letter.

1	2	3
f h g	m h s	f s m
4	5	6
h m f	m g s	s h g
7	8	9
g f m	s h f	g s h
10	11	12
m h s	f g h	m g h

Harcourt Brace School Publishers

Name _____

REVIEW

Say the name of each picture. Write the letter that stands for its beginning sound. Then trace the whole word.

1	2	3
mat	at	ork
4	5	6
un	irl	ap
7	8	9
ill	op	ame
10	11	12
ox	um	aw

Name _____

Say the name of each picture. If it begins with the same sound as **turtle,** write **Tt** on the lines.

turtle

Harcourt Brace School Publishers

Say the name of each picture. Color the pictures whose names begin with the same sound as  .

Name _____

car

Say the name of each picture. If it begins with the same sound as **car**, write **C c** on the lines.

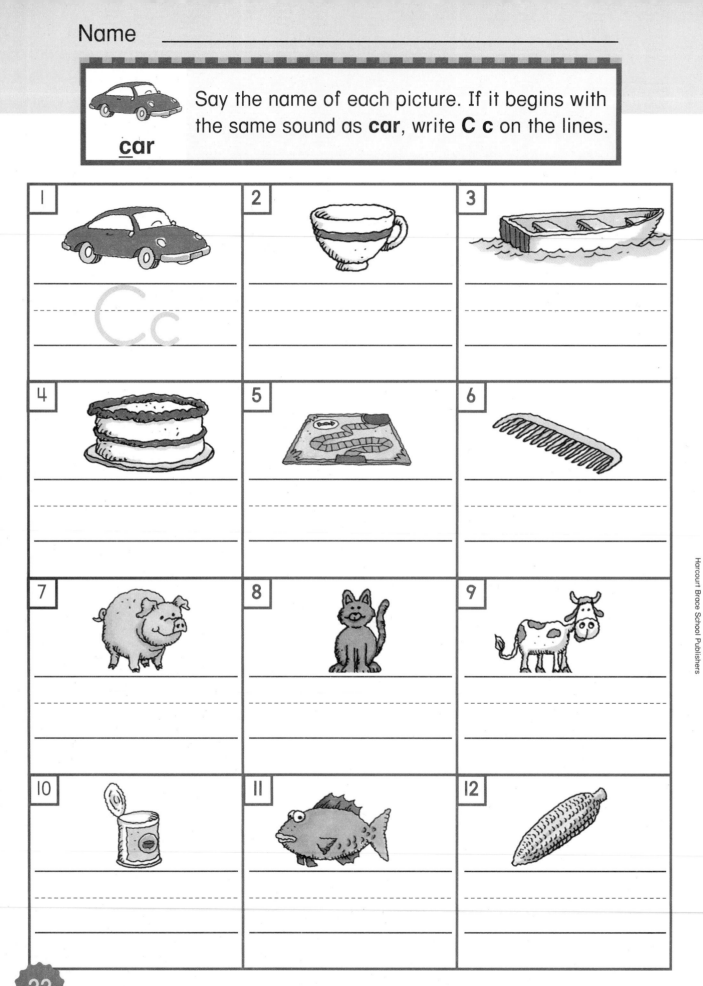

1.

2.

3.

4.

5.

6.

7.

8.

9.

10.

11.

12.

Name _____

Say the name of each picture. Color the pictures whose names begin with the same sound as  .

Initial Consonant: / r / • Phonemic Awareness

Name _____

Say the name of each picture. If it begins with the same sound as **raccoon,** write **Rr** on the lines.

_raccoon

1.

2.

3.

4.

5.

6.

7.

8.

9.

10.

11.

12.

Harcourt Brace School Publishers

Name _____

Say the name of each picture. Color the pictures whose names begin with the same sound as .

Initial Consonant: / b / • Phonemic Awareness

Name _____

ball

Say the name of each picture. If it begins with the same sound as **ball**, write **Bb** on the lines.

Initial Consonant: / b / b

Phonics Practice Book

Say the name of each picture. Color the pictures whose names begin with the same sound as  .

Name _____

lamp

Say the name of each picture. If it begins with the same sound as **lamp**, write **Ll** on the lines.

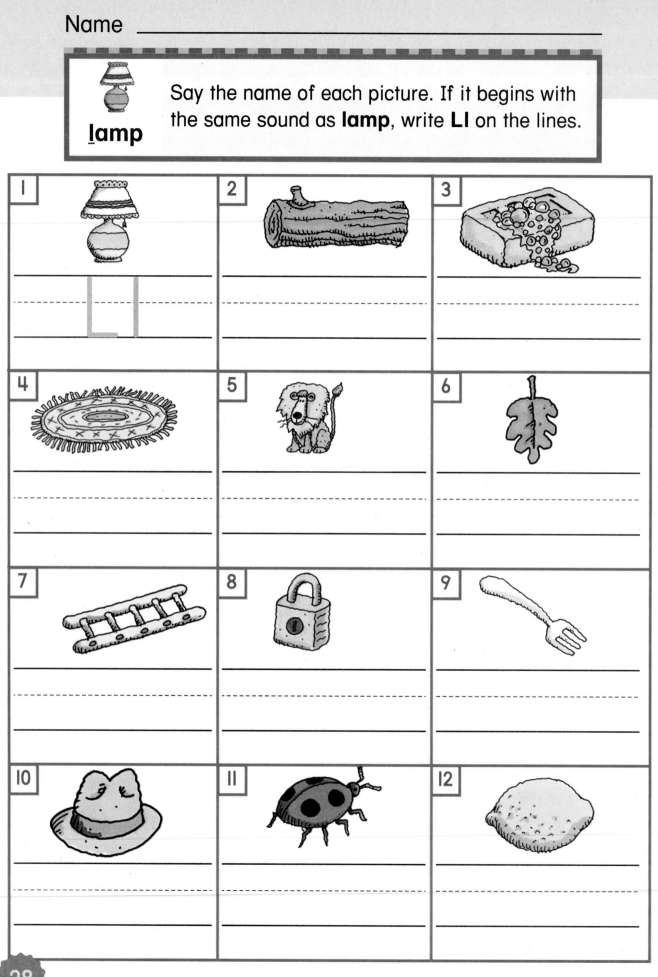

1	2	3
4	5	6
7	8	9
10	11	12

Initial Consonant: / l / l   Phonics Practice Book

Harcourt Brace School Publishers

Name _____

Say the name of each picture. Circle its beginning letter.

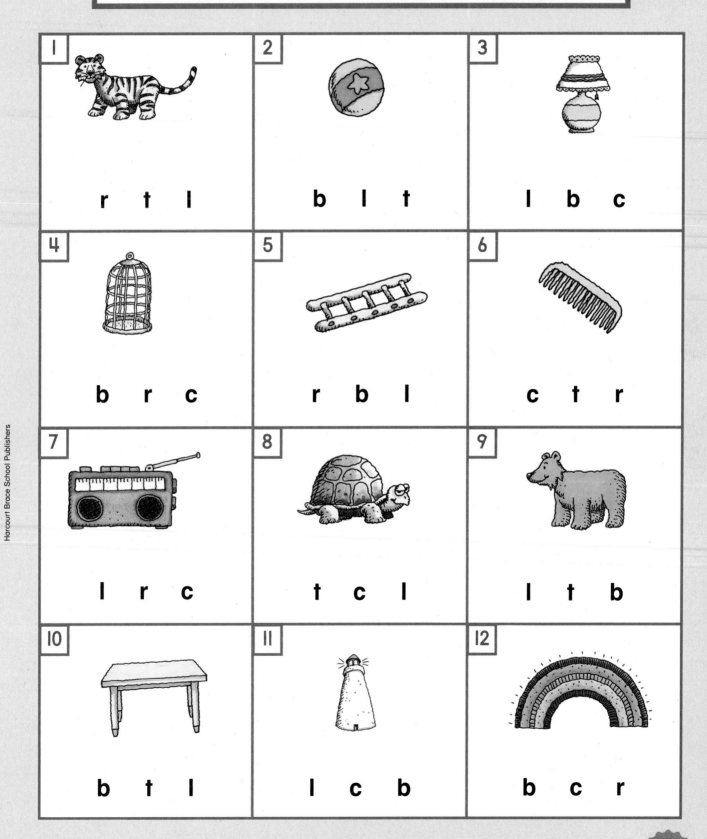

1	**2**	**3**
r t l	b l t	l b c
4	**5**	**6**
b r c	r b l	c t r
7	**8**	**9**
l r c	t c l	l t b
10	**11**	**12**
b t l	l c b	b c r

Name _____

REVIEW

Say the name of each picture. Write the letter that stands for its beginning sound. Then trace the whole word.

1	2	3
tree	up	ell
4	**5**	**6**
ake	ox	id
7	**8**	**9**
ike	ow	ing
10	**11**	**12**
og	ug	en

Harcourt Brace School Publishers

Review of Initial Consonants: / t / t, / k / c, / r / r, / b / b, / l / l

Phonics Practice Book

Name _____

yak

Help the  get home. Color the pictures whose names begin with the same sound as .

Harcourt Brace School Publishers

Name _____

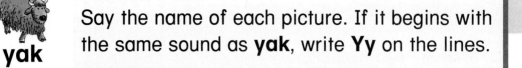

yak

Say the name of each picture. If it begins with the same sound as **yak**, write **Yy** on the lines.

Initial Consonant: / y / y

Harcourt Brace School Publishers

Name _____

Say the name of each picture. Color the pictures whose names begin with the same sound as .

Name _____

duck

Say the name of each picture. If it begins with the same sound as **duck**, write **Dd** on the lines.

Harcourt Brace School Publishers

Say the name of each picture. Color the pictures whose names begin with the same sound as 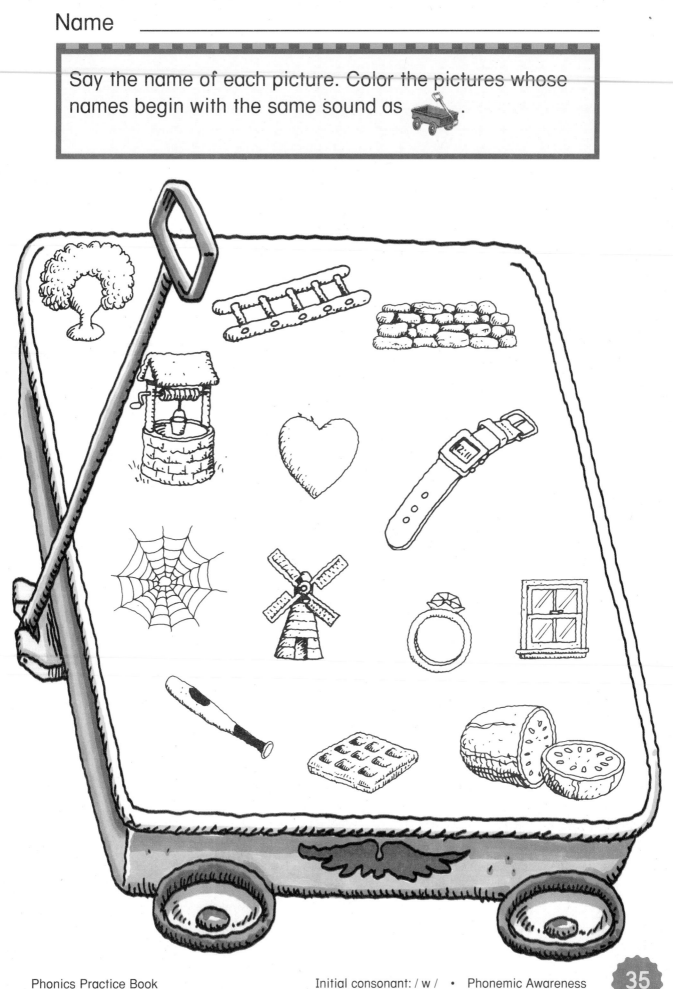.

Name _____

wagon

Say the name of each picture. If it begins with the same sound as **wagon**, write **Ww** on the lines.

1	2	3

4	5	6

7	8	9

10	11	12

Initial Consonant: / w / w

Phonics Practice Book

Harcourt Brace School Publishers

Name _____

Say the name of each picture. Color the pictures whose names begin with the same sound as 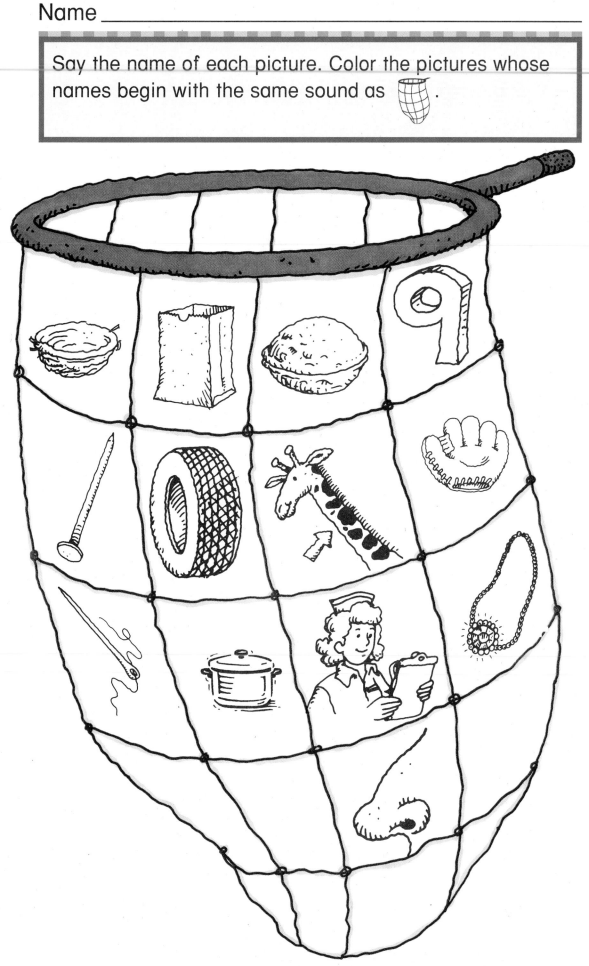 .

Name _____

net

Say the name of each picture. If it begins with the same sound as **net**, write **Nn** on the lines.

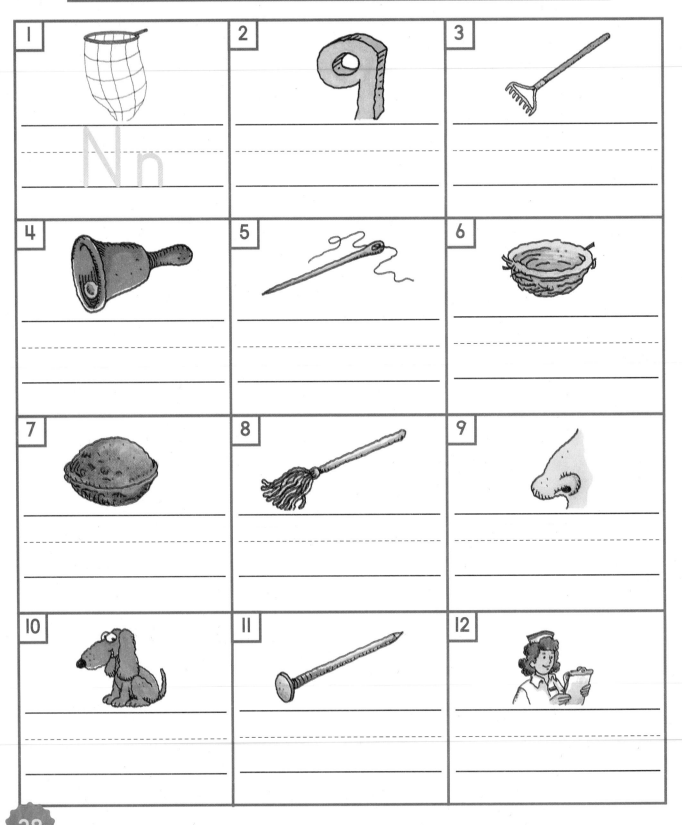

Initial Consonant: / n / n

Name _____

Say the name of each picture. Color the pictures whose names begin with the same sound as  .

Initial Consonant: / p / • Phonemic Awareness

Name _____

pig

Say the name of each picture. If it begins with the same sound as **pig**, write **P p** on the lines.

1	2	3
4	5	6
7	8	9
10	11	12

Initial Consonant: / p / p

Phonics Practice Book

Harcourt Brace School Publishers

Name _____

Say the name of each picture. Circle its beginning letter.

1	2	3
n y w	n w y	p n d
4	5	6
n p d	d w n	n y p
7	8	9
w y p	d w n	w y p
10	11	12
w d y	n w d	p d n

Harcourt Brace School Publishers

Name _____

Say the name of each picture. Write the letter that stands for its beginning sound. Then trace the whole word.

1 nail	**2** ig	**3** esk
4 ard	**5** ig	**6** oll
7 an	**8** eck	**9** ak
10 og	**11** izza	**12** atch

Review of Initial Consonants: / y / y, / d / d, / w / w, / n / n, / p / p

Phonics Practice Book

Name _____

Help the  get the _____. Color the pictures whose names begin with the same sound as _____.

Initial Consonant: / z / • Phonemic Awareness

Name _____

zebra

Say the name of each picture. If it begins with the same sound as **zebra,** write **Zz** on the lines.

Initial Consonant: / z / z

Harcourt Brace School Publishers

Name _____

Say the name of each picture. Color the pictures whose names begin with the same sound as  .

Name _____

kite

Say the name of each picture. If it begins with the same sound as **kite**, write **Kk** on the lines.

Initial Consonant / k / k

Phonics Practice Book

Harcourt Brace School Publishers

Say the name of each picture. Color the pictures whose names begin with the same sound as 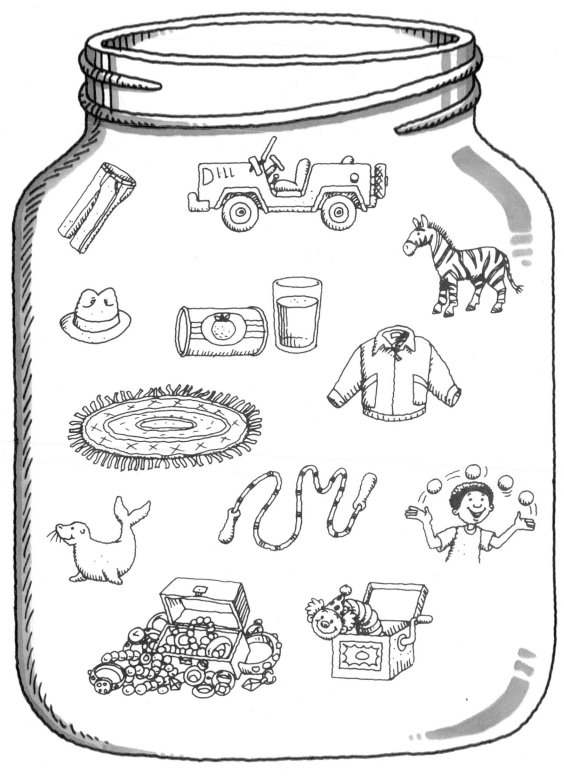.

Name _____

jar

Say the name of each picture. If it begins with the same sound as **jar**, write **Jj** on the lines.

Initial Consonant: / j / j

Harcourt Brace School Publishers

Phonics Practice Book

Say the name of each picture. Color the pictures whose names begin with the same sound as  .

Name _____

_van

Say the name of each picture. If it begins with the same sound as **van,** write **Vv** on the lines.

Initial Consonant: / v /: v

Phonics Practice Book

Harcourt Brace School Publishers

Name _____

Say the name of each picture. Circle its beginning letter.

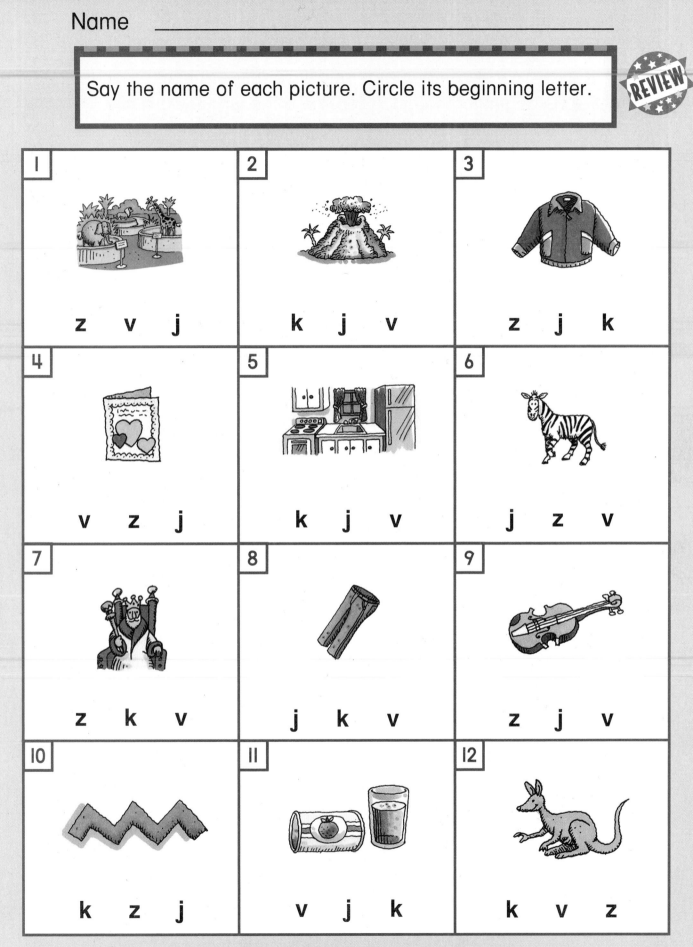

1 z v **j**

2 k **j** v

3 z **j** k

4 **v** z j

5 **k** j v

6 j **z** v

7 z **k** v

8 j **k** v

9 z j **v**

10 k **z** j

11 **v** j k

12 **k** v z

Name _____

Say the name of each picture. Write the letter that stands for its beginning sound. Then trace the whole word.

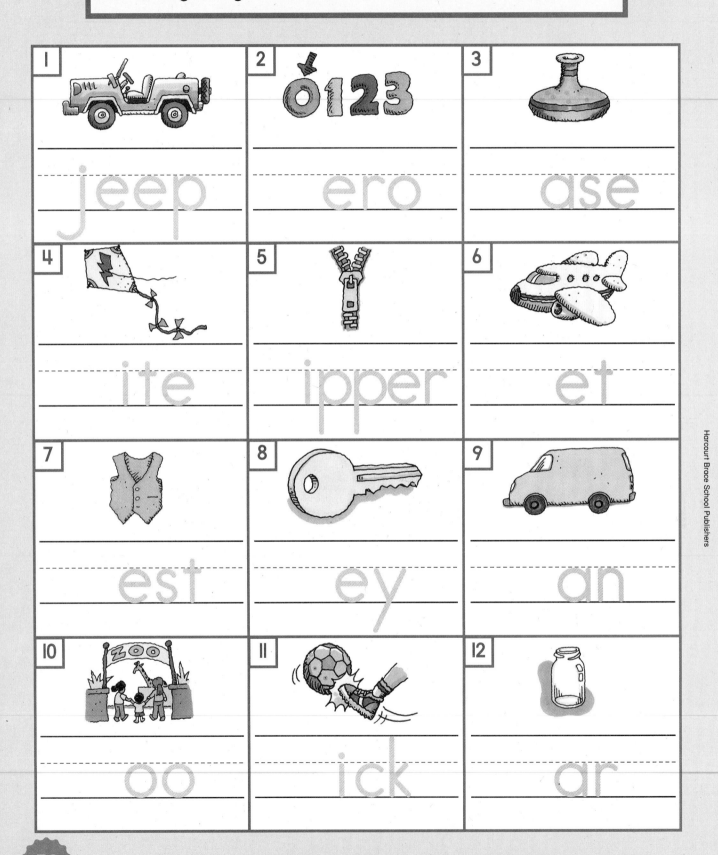

1. _____ jeep

2. _____ ero

3. _____ ase

4. _____ ite

5. _____ ipper

6. _____ et

7. _____ est

8. _____ ey

9. _____ an

10. _____ oo

11. _____ ick

12. _____ ar

Review of Initial Consonants: / z / z, / k / k, / j / j, / v / v

Phonics Practice Book

Harcourt Brace School Publishers

Name _____

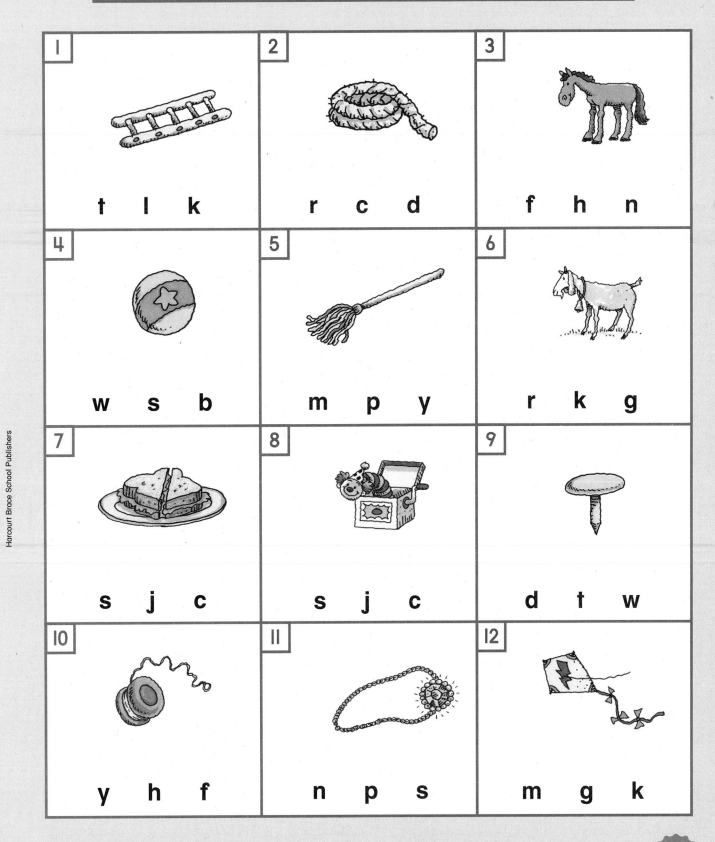

1	**2**	**3**
t l k	r c d	f h n
4	**5**	**6**
w s b	m p y	r k g
7	**8**	**9**
s j c	s j c	d t w
10	**11**	**12**
y h f	n p s	m g k

Name _____

Say the name of each picture. Write the letter that stands for its beginning sound. Then trace the whole word.

1 ish	2 oll	3 eb
4 at	5 at	6 est
7 an	8 ing	9 un
10 en	11 ap	12 am

Cumulative Review of Initial Consonants   Phonics Practice Book

Harcourt Brace School Publishers

Name _____

Write the letter that stands for the beginning sound of each picture's name.

1 C	2	3
4	5	6
7	8	9
10	11	12

CHECK-UP

Write the letter that stands for the beginning sound of each picture's name.

Harcourt Brace School Publishers

Name _____

1. cub

2. can

Harcourt Brace School Publishers

Name _____

Say the name of the picture in the box. Color the pictures whose names end with the same sound.

1

cat

2

cap

Final Consonants: / t / t, / p / p

Phonics Practice Book

Name _____

Say the name of each picture. Circle the letter that stands for its ending sound.

1.
t　n　b

2.
p　t　n

3.
n　t　b

4.
t　b　p

5.
b　t　n

6.
t　n　b

7.
b　n　t

8.
t　n　p

9.
n　t　p

10.
t　n　b

11.
p　n　t

12.
b　t　n

Name _____

Write the letter that completes each picture name. Then trace the whole word.

(b n t p)

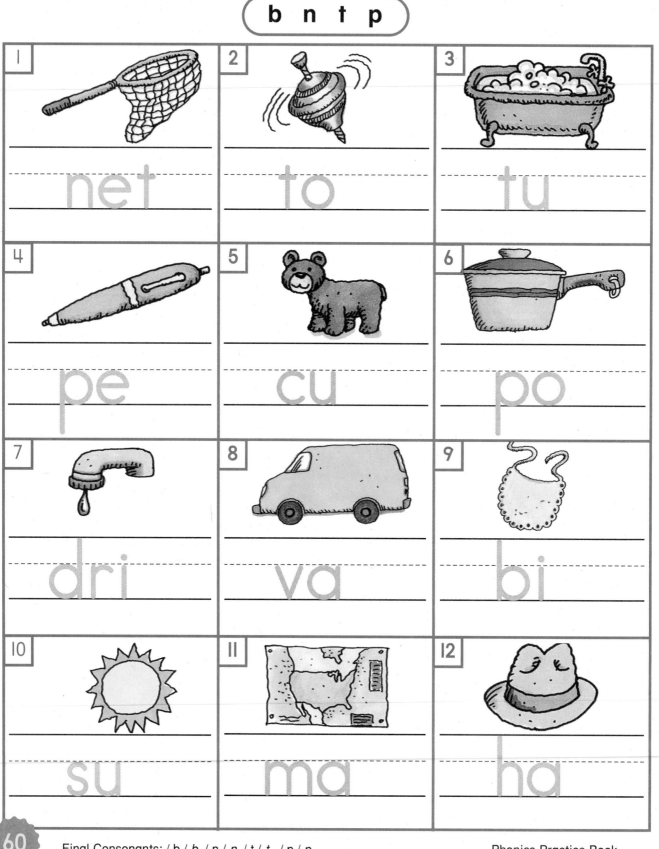

1. net
2. to
3. tu
4. pe
5. cu
6. po
7. dri
8. va
9. bi
10. su
11. ma
12. ha

Final Consonants: / b / b, / n / n, / t / t, / p / p

Harcourt Brace School Publishers

Phonics Practice Book

duck

book

Color the pictures whose names end with the same sound as **duck** and **book**.

Final Consonants: / k / *k, ck*

61

Name _____

1

seal

ball

2

pig

egg

Final Consonants: / l / *l*, *ll*; / g / *g*, *gg*

Phonics Practice Book

Harcourt Brace School Publishers

Name _____

Say the name of each picture. Circle the letter or letters that stand for its ending sound.

1. ck   gg   ll

2. g   l   k

3. ll   ck   g

4. k   g   l

5. g   l   k

6. ck   gg   ll

7. ll   gg   ck

8. l   g   k

9. l   k   g

10. ll   ck   gg

11. g   k   l

12. ck   ll   gg

Name _____

Say the name of each picture. Circle and write the letter or letters that stand for its ending sound. Then trace the whole word.

1. g   k   l

bag

2. l   g   k

boo

3. ck   ll   gg

be

4. ck   gg   ll

du

5. gg   ck   ll

e

6. k   l   g

sea

7. ll   gg   ck

hi

8. gg   ck   ll

ta

9. k   l   g

pi

Harcourt Brace School Publishers

Final Consonants: / k / k, ck; / l / l, ll; / g / g, / gg

Say the name of each picture. Circle the letter or letters that stand for its ending sound.

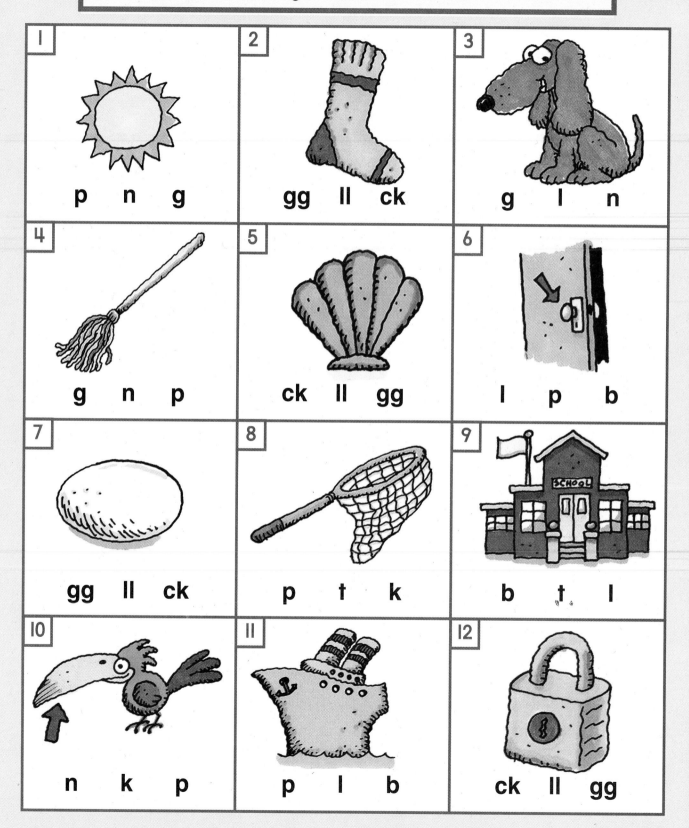

1 p n g

2 gg ll ck

3 g l n

4 g n p

5 ck ll gg

6 l p b

7 gg ll ck

8 p t k

9 b t l

10 n k p

11 p l b

12 ck ll gg

Name _____

My Dog Jack

My big dog Jack
Ran away from the cat.
He climbed in a sack.
Then he sat on my hat.

Jack comes when I call.
He finds me my ball.
Jack is the dog
I like best of all.

What did you learn about Jack?

_____

- -

_____

_____

- -

_____

Harcourt Brace School Publishers

Name _____

Say the name of the picture in the box. Color the pictures whose names end with the same sound.

1

o**x**

2

ja**m**

Harcourt Brace School Publishers

Name _____

pa<u>d</u>

Color the pictures whose names end with the same sound as **pad.**

Final Consonant: / d / d

Phonics Practice Book

Name _____

Say the name of each picture. Circle the letter that stands for its ending sound.

1	2	3
x m d	m x d	d x m

4	5	6
x d m	d x m	d m x

7	8	9
x d m	m x d	m x d

10	11	12
x d m	x m d	m x d

Name _____

Write the letter from the box that completes each picture name. Then trace the whole word.

x   m   d

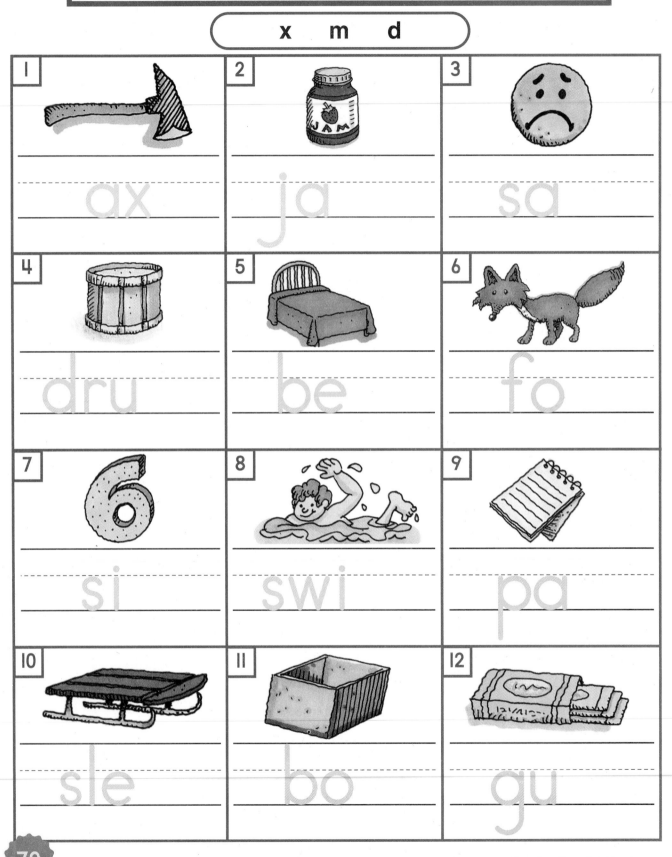

1	2	3
ax	ja	sa
4	5	6
dru	be	fo
7	8	9
si	swi	pa
10	11	12
sle	bo	gu

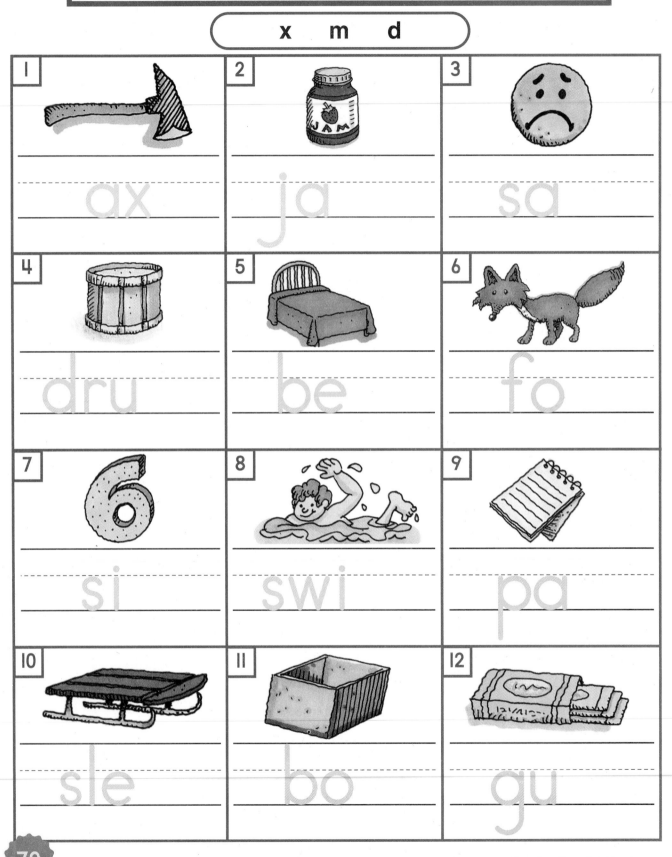

Final Consonants: / ks / x, / m / m, / d / d

Phonics Practice Book

Name _____

Color the pictures whose names end like the first picture or pictures in the box.

1

bees

buzz

2

hoof

puff

Harcourt Brace School Publishers

Final Consonants: / z / s, zz; / f / f, ff

Name _____

Say the name of each picture. Circle and write the letter or letters that stand for its ending sound. Then trace the whole word.

1 s f n lea	**2** f m s cow	**3** zz ll ff cu
4 ff zz ck bu	**5** t f s key	**6** f g s roo
7 zz gg ff o	**8** l s f eye	**9** f s d shoe

Harcourt Brace School Publishers

Final Consonants: / z / s, zz; / f / f, ff

Phonics Practice Book

Name _____

Color each picture whose name ends like the first picture or pictures in the box.

Final Consonants: / d / *dd;* / t / *tt;* / s / *s, ss*

Name _____

Say the name of each picture. Circle and write the letter or letters that stand for its ending sound. Then trace the whole word.

1

dd   ff   tt

mi

2

f   s   x

ga

3

ff   ss   dd

gla

4

ss   dd   ff

ki

5

ff   ss   dd

dre

6

dd   tt   ll

a

7

dd   tt   ss

gra

8

p   s   d

bu

9

m   f   s

plu

Final Consonants: / d / *dd*; / t / *tt*; / s / *s, ss*

Phonics Practice Book

Name _____

Say the name of each picture. Circle the letter or letters that stand for its ending sound.

1. f　m　x

2. dd　ff　zz

3. d　m　x

4. s　d　m

5. tt　dd　ff

6. d　m　f

7. x　d　s

8. ff　zz　ss

9. ff　tt　dd

10. x　s　d

11. tt　ff　ss

12. f　d　m

Name_____

REVIEW

Say the name of each picture. Circle and write the letter or letters that stand for its ending sound. Then trace the whole word.

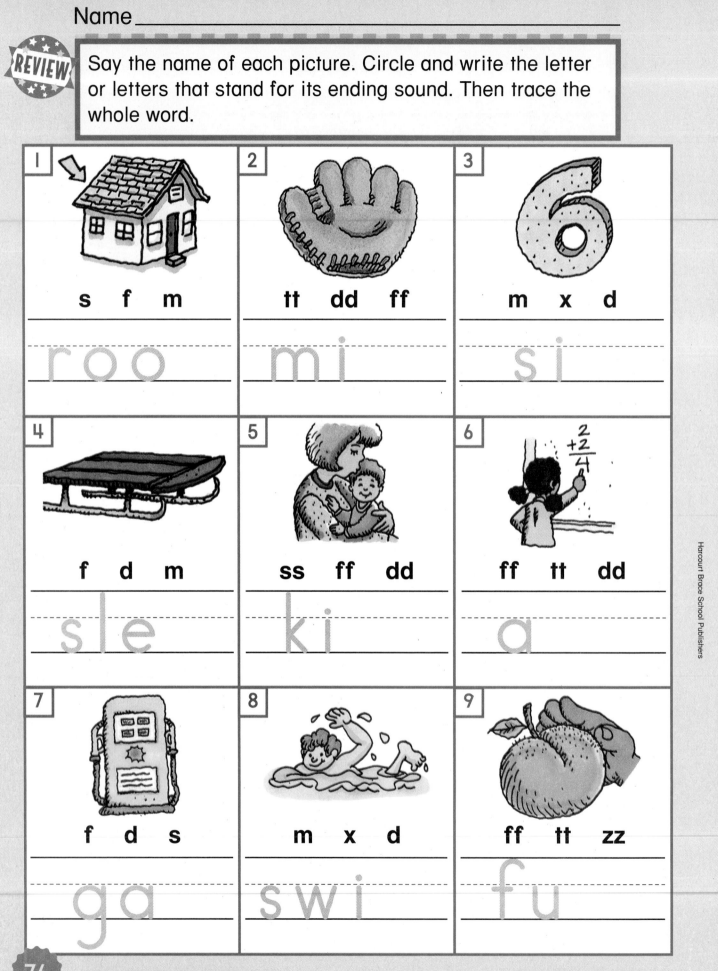

1.

s   f   m

r o o ____

2.

tt   dd   ff

m i ____

3.

m   x   d

s i ____

4.

f   d   m

s l e ____

5.

ss   ff   dd

k i ____

6.

ff   tt   dd

a ____

7.

f   d   s

g a ____

8.

m   x   d

s w i ____

9.

ff   tt   zz

f u ____

76

Review of Final Consonants

Phonics Practice Book

Harcourt Brace School Publishers

Name _____

Read the poem. Then use a word from the poem to complete each sentence.

Duck Trouble

The duck said, "Quack, quack!
I sat on a tack."
The toad gave a big croak
and said, "That's not a joke!"
Buzz-buzz went the bees
from up in the trees.
"Too bad," said a frog
from his leaf in the fog.

_____

1. The duck sat on a _____ .

2. The toad gave a big _____ .

3. The bees were flying in the _____ .

4. The frog was sitting on a _____ .

Harcourt Brace School Publishers

Name _____

Say the name of each picture. Circle the letter or letters that stand for its ending sound.

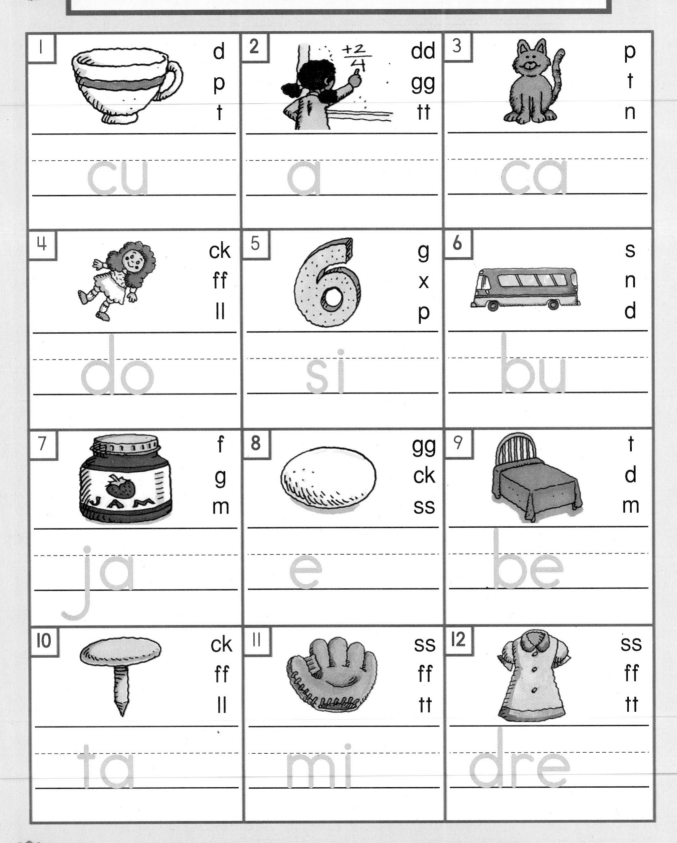

1. d p t

cu____

2. dd gg tt

a____

3. p t n

ca____

4. ck ff ll

do____

5. g x p

si____

6. s n d

bu____

7. f g m

ja____

8. gg ck ss

e____

9. t d m

be____

10. ck ff ll

ta____

11. ss ff tt

mi____

12. ss ff tt

dre____

Harcourt Brace School Publishers

Name _____

Write the word that makes each sentence tell about the picture.

(pepper rabbit better jelly carrot)

1	What did the
	_____

	_____ find?

2	
	_____

	It is a big _____.

3	Will you have
	_____

	_____ on it?

4	Will you have it with
	_____

	_____ ?

5	No, I like it
	_____

	_____ like this!

Name _____

Write the word that completes each sentence.

carry   ladder   hello   happy

1

Here comes a man with a

_____

_____ .

2

_____

He will _____ it
and then climb up.

3

Now we can go. We are

_____

_____ .

4

_____

Then we said _____
to Mother.

Double Consonants   Phonics Practice Book

Harcourt Brace School Publishers

Name _____

Write the letter that completes each picture name. Then trace the whole word.

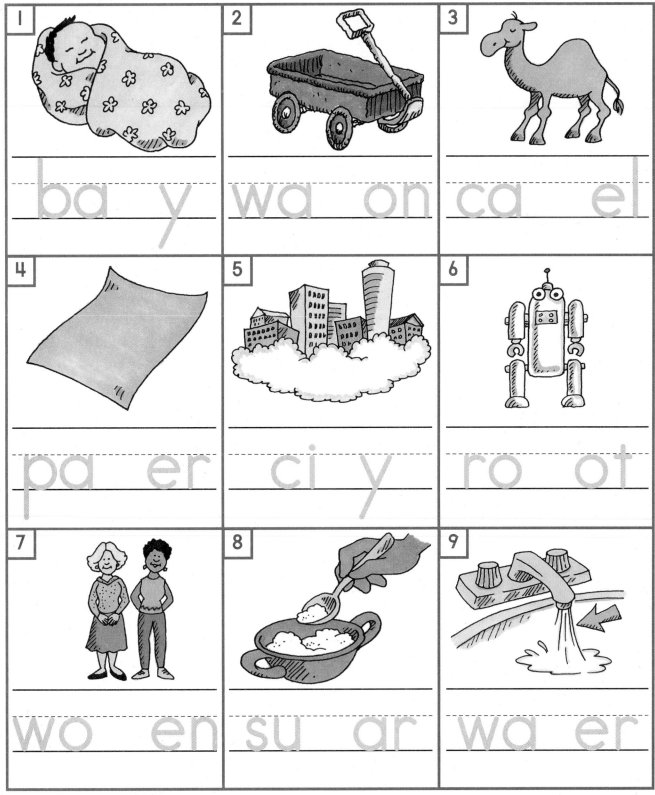

1. ba __ y

2. wa __ on

3. ca __ el

4. pa __ er

5. ci __ y

6. ro __ ot

7. wo __ en

8. su __ ar

9. wa __ er

Look at each picture. Circle the word that completes the sentence. Then write the word.

1	I like this _____ - - - - - - - - - - - - _____ .	wagon wanted willow
2	My mother mixes lemons, sugar _____ - - - - - - - - - - - - and _____ .	women window water
3	_____ - - - - - - - - - - - - We are _____ to get wet!	away about any
4	_____ - - - - - - - - - - - - I want blue _____ for my robot.	pencil paper pony
5	We can ride a tiger and a _____ - - - - - - - - - - - - _____ .	color cupcake camel

Medial Consonants: / b / b, / g / g, / m / m, / p / p, / t / t

Phonics Practice Book

Say the name of each picture. Write the letter that completes the word. Then trace the whole word.

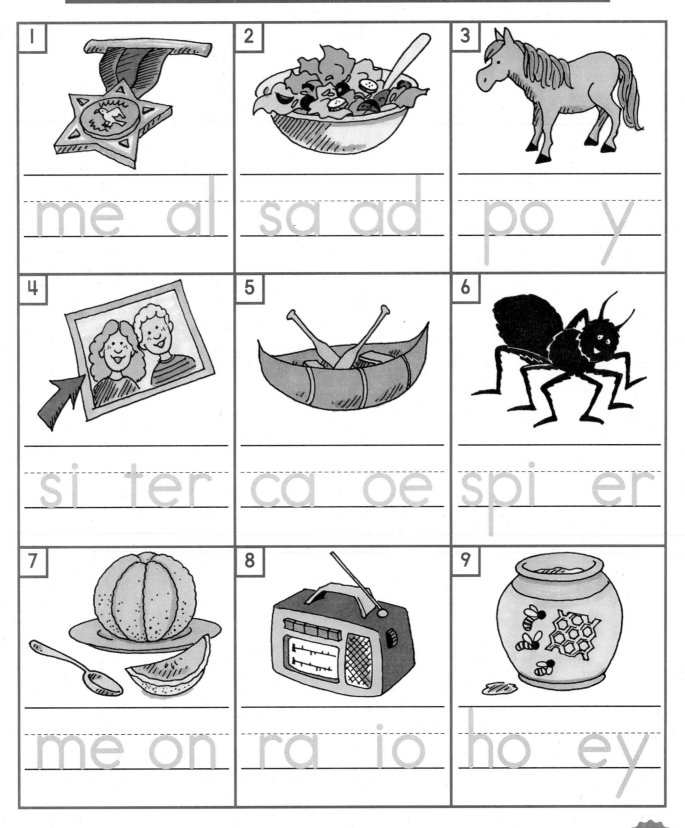

1. me __ al

2. sa __ ad

3. po __ y

4. si __ ter

5. ca __ oe

6. spi __ er

7. me __ on

8. ra __ io

9. ho __ ey

Name _____

Look at each picture. Circle the word that completes the sentence. Then write the word.

1	Wow! Look at this _____ _____ _____ .	giggle garden gazelle
2	_____ _____ This _____ must like to dig.	pony pencil person
3	Look at that big _____ _____ _____ .	spider supper sister
4	Those bees make lots of _____ _____ _____ .	holly happy honey
5	Would you boys like to pick some _____ _____ _____ greens?	story salad surprise

Medial Consonants: / d / d, / l / l, / n / n, / s / s

Name _____

Circle and write the letter or letters that complete each picture name. Then trace the whole word.

1. **gg** **ck** **tt**

du

2. **t** **l** **b**

ci y

3. **k** **g** **x**

fo

4. **ff** **pp** **ll**

ba oon

5. **g** **k** **n**

pi

6. **zz** **ss** **dd**

gla

7. **p** **g** **m**

ti er

8. **ck** **ff** **dd**

la er

9. **g** **p** **b**

bi

Harcourt Brace School Publishers

Name _____

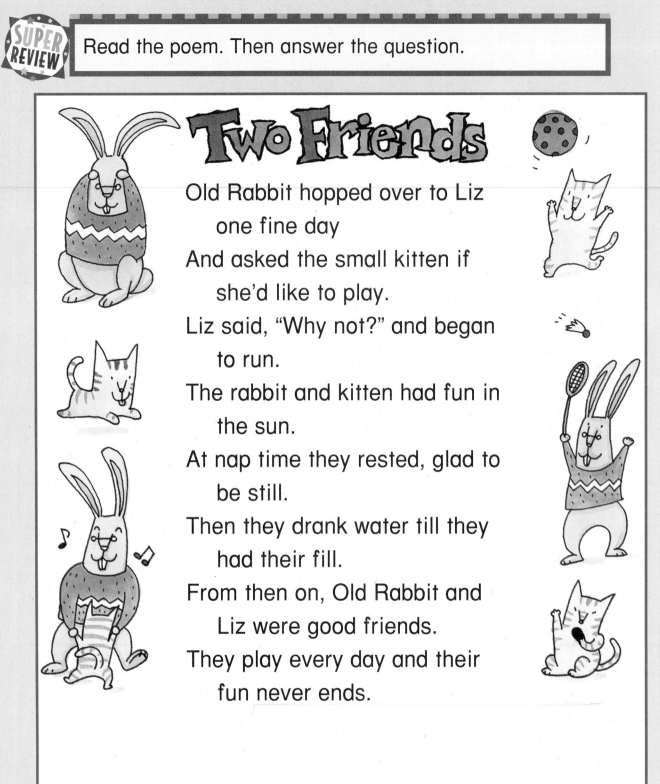

Two Friends

Old Rabbit hopped over to Liz
    one fine day
And asked the small kitten if
    she'd like to play.
Liz said, "Why not?" and began
    to run.
The rabbit and kitten had fun in
    the sun.
At nap time they rested, glad to
    be still.
Then they drank water till they
    had their fill.
From then on, Old Rabbit and
    Liz were good friends.
They play every day and their
    fun never ends.

Harcourt Brace School Publishers

What do Old Rabbit and Liz do that you and your friends do?

_____

- -

_____

Name _____

Fill in the circle next to the letter or letters that complete each picture name. Write the letters. Then trace the whole word.

CHECK-UP

1. ○ d ○ p ○ t

cu _____

2. ○ tt ○ dd ○ ss

mi _____

3. ○ t ○ d ○ l

mai _____

4. ○ m ○ d ○ n

spi _____ er

5. ○ pp ○ ss ○ ff

ha _____ y

6. ○ n ○ p ○ m

ca _____ el

7. ○ m ○ d ○ n

fa _____

8. ○ p ○ l ○ n

pa _____ er

9. ○ dd ○ ff ○ zz

o _____

10. ○ m ○ b ○ n

dru _____

11. ○ ss ○ bb ○ ff

ra _____ it

12. ○ m ○ f ○ k

boo _____

Look at the pictures. Draw a line from the sentence to the picture it tells about.

1

Tony gets the mail.

Mark pets the cat.

Jack rides the sled.

2

The girls played catch.

The girls went in.

The girls found an egg.

3

Bees buzz by the truck.

Bees buzz in the road.

Bees buzz over grass.

4

A lemon is on a branch.

A carrot fell down.

A melon began to grow.

Harcourt Brace School Publishers

Name _____

Say the name of the first picture in each row. Circle the pictures whose names rhyme with it.

Name _____

Say the names of the pictures in each row. Color the pictures whose names rhyme.

Short Vowel: / a / • Phonemic Awareness

Phonics Practice Book

Harcourt Brace School Publishers

Color the pictures whose names have the sound you hear at the beginning of  and in the middle of 🐱 .

Harcourt Brace School Publishers

Name _____

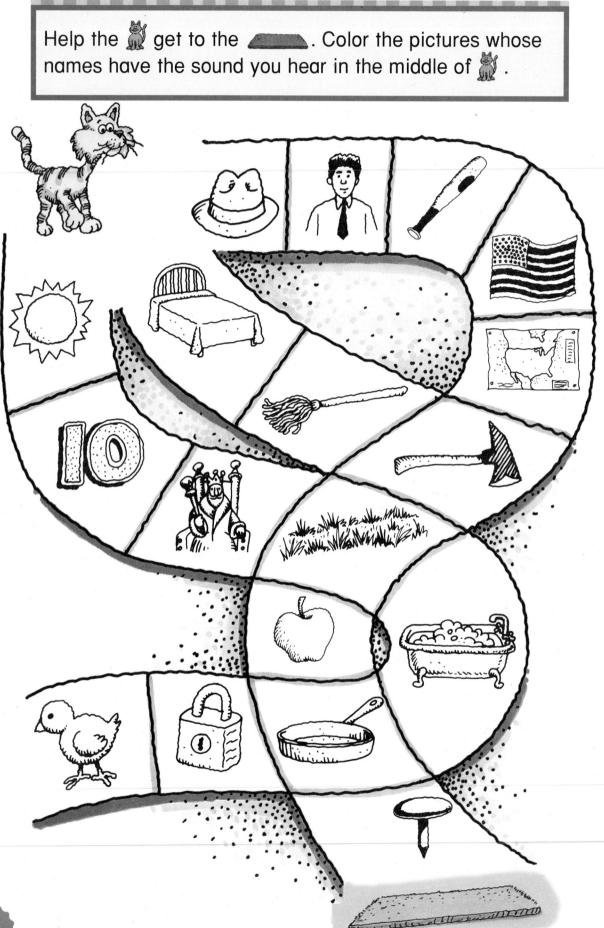

Short Vowel: / a / • Phonemic Awareness

Phonics Practice Book

Harcourt Brace School Publishers

Name _____

Color the pictures whose names have the sound you hear at the beginning of 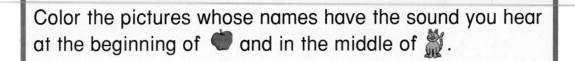 and in the middle of .

Draw three things that rhyme with .

cat

Write **a** under each word that has the sound you hear in the middle of **cat.**

1.

2.

3.

4.

5.

6.

7.

8.

9.

10.

11.

12.

Short Vowel: / a / a

Harcourt Brace School Publishers

Phonics Practice Book

Name _____

Write **a** to complete each picture name that has the sound you hear in the middle of **cat**. Then trace the whole word.

1. van	2. s __ d	3. b __ d
4. b __ g	5. d __ g	6. b __ t
7. b __ g	8. p __ n	9. d __ d
10. c __ p	11. p __ n	12. f __ n

Short Vowel: / a / a

Name _____

clap

Write four words that rhyme with **clap.** Then color the pictures.

1

tap

2

3

4

Name _____

Write the word that names each picture.

cap   nap   map   lap   tap

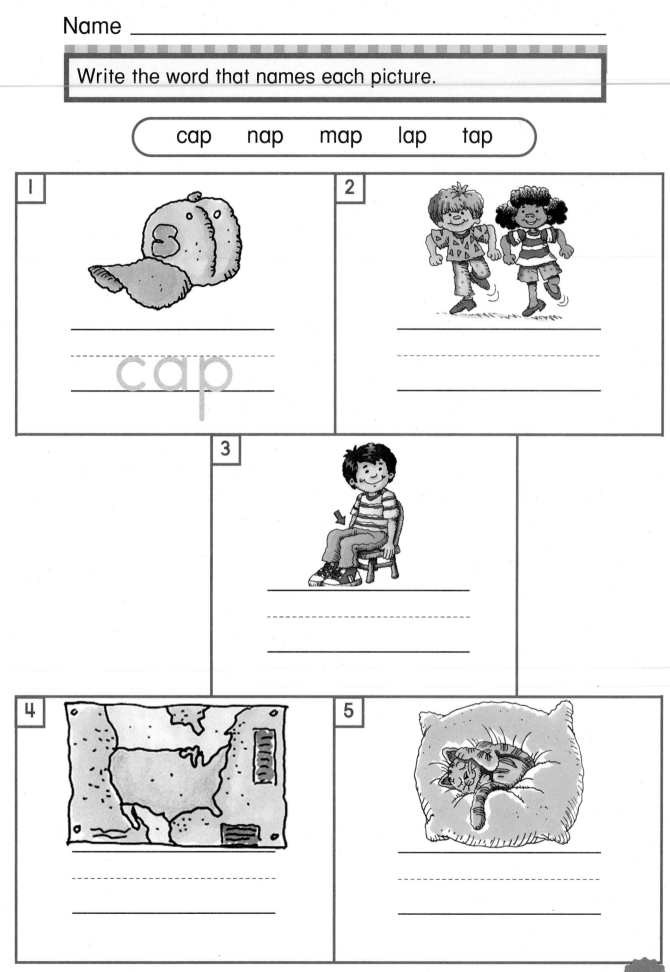

1.
cap

2.
_____

3.
_____

4.
_____

5.
_____

Name _____

Circle the word that completes each sentence. Then write
the word.

1	The dog can _____.	nap hands
2	I said, "Jump in _____ my _____."	can lap
3	"Find my _____!"	tap hands
4	The dog likes _____ the _____.	can map
5	"Oh no! Not my _____ _____!"	cap and

Short Vowel: / a / a • Reading Words with Short a   Phonics Practice Book

Name _____

Say the names of the pictures in each row. Color the pictures whose names rhyme.

Name _____

Color the pictures whose names have the sound you hear in the middle of  .

Short Vowel: / o / • Phonemic Awareness

Phonics Practice Book

Name _____

f_ox

Write **o** to complete each picture name that has the sound you hear in the middle of **fox.** Then trace the whole word.

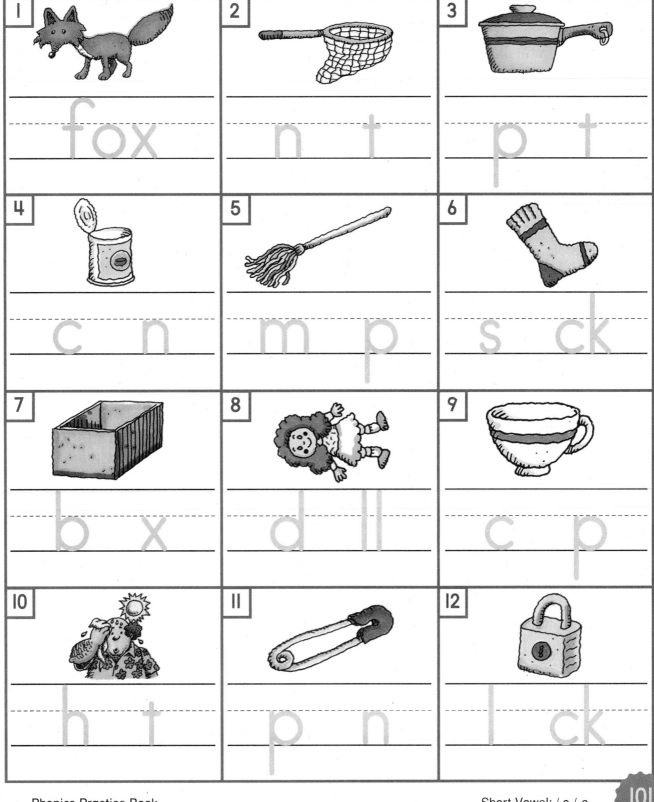

1 — fox —	2 — n _ t —	3 — p _ t —
4 — c _ n —	5 — m _ p —	6 — s _ ck —
7 — b _ x —	8 — d _ ll —	9 — c _ p —
10 — h _ t —	11 — p _ n —	12 — l _ ck —

Short Vowel: / o / o   **101**

Name _____

1. fox

2.

3.

4.

5.

6.

Short Vowel: / o / o • Writing Words with Short o

Phonics Practice Book

Harcourt Brace School Publishers

Name _____

STOP

stop

Write the picture names that rhyme with **stop**.
Then add one more rhyming word and picture.

1

_____

top

2

_____

3

_____

4

_____

Name _____

1. h o t

2. t o p

3. c o t

4. m o p

5. p o t

Short Vowel: / o / o • Blending

Phonics Practice Book

Harcourt Brace School Publishers

Write **o** to complete each word. Trace the whole word.
Then draw a picture of the word.

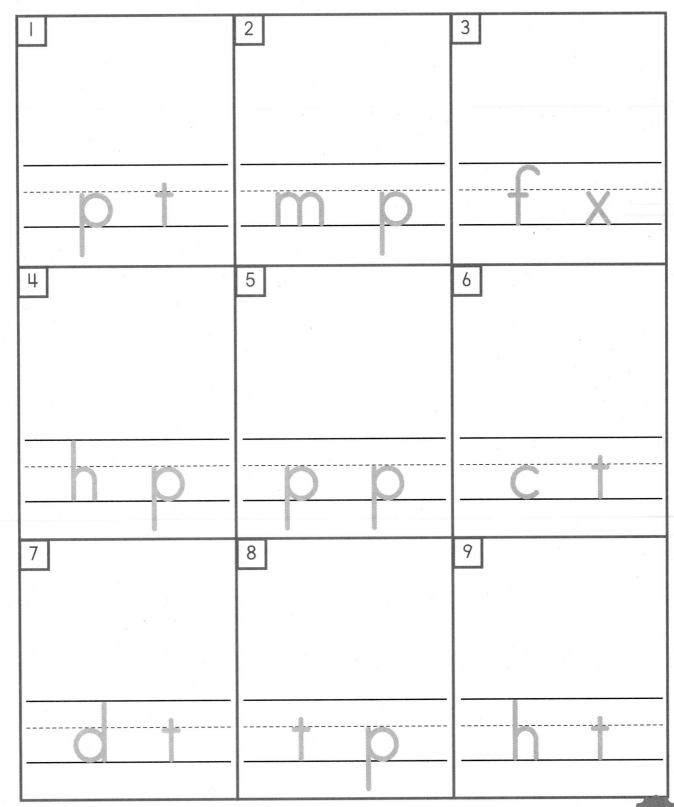

1. p _ t

2. m _ p

3. f _ x

4. h _ p

5. p _ p

6. c _ t

7. d _ t

8. t _ p

9. h _ t

Short Vowel: / o / o • Reading Words with Short o

Name _____

Look at each picture. Write the word from the box that completes the sentence.

| hot | got | hop | top | job | cot |

1		_____ - - - - - - - - - - - - - - - I can _____ .
2		_____ - - - - - - - - - - - - - - - Todd will do the _____ .
3		_____ - - - - - - - - - - - - - - - The sun is _____ .
4		_____ - - - - - - - - - - - - - - - I have a _____ .
5		_____ - - - - - - - - - - - - - - - It is on the _____ .
6		_____ - - - - - - - - - - - - - - - The pig _____ down.

Short Vowel: / o / o • Reading Words with Short o

Phonics Practice Book

Circle the sentence that tells about each picture.

1	You can see Bob jump. You can hop in. You can see the mop.
2	See me hop. See me sob. See me on the cot.
3	I have a big dog. I did not see it. It was on top.
4	Bob sees the dog. Bob did the job. Bob is jumping.
5	I will hop on the cot. I will find a big pot. I will pop the top.
6	It is in the pot. It is a big dot. It is not hot.

Name _____

Write the word from the box that completes each sentence.

top job lot mop pot got

1

Nan climbed

up and

_____

- - - - - - - - - - - - - - -

_____

the big can.

2

Bob will go find

the big

_____

- - - - - - - - - - - - - - -

_____ .

3

Dot has a big

_____

- - - - - - - - - - - - - - -

_____!

4

Don likes it a

_____

- - - - - - - - - - - - - - -

_____!

5

The dog

jumped up on

_____

- - - - - - - - - - - - - - -

_____ .

6

Don said, "I will

_____

- - - - - - - - - - - - - - -

_____

it up."

Short Vowel: / o / o • Reading Words with Short o

Phonics Practice Book

Name _____

Write **a** or **o** to complete each picture name. Then trace the whole word.

1. m __ p

2. c __ t

3. p __ t

4. f __ n

5. t __ p

6. c __ p

7. h __ t

8. m __ t

9. c __ n

10. c __ t

11. v __ n

12. h __ p

REVIEW

Read the story, and answer the question.

What Is It?

"What have you got in the big pot?" said Bob.

"It can hop on your lap," said Ann.

"It will come if you clap."

"Is it fat?" said Bob.

"It is not," said Ann.

"Do you want to see it?

It will hop out."

"It's a dog!" said Bob.

What is in the pot?

_____

- -

_____

Harcourt Brace School Publishers

Name _____

Short Vowel: / e / • Phonemic Awareness

111

Say the name of each picture. Color the pictures whose names have the sound you hear in the middle of .

Name _____

bell

Write **e** to complete each picture name that has the sound you hear in the middle of **bell**. Then trace the whole word.

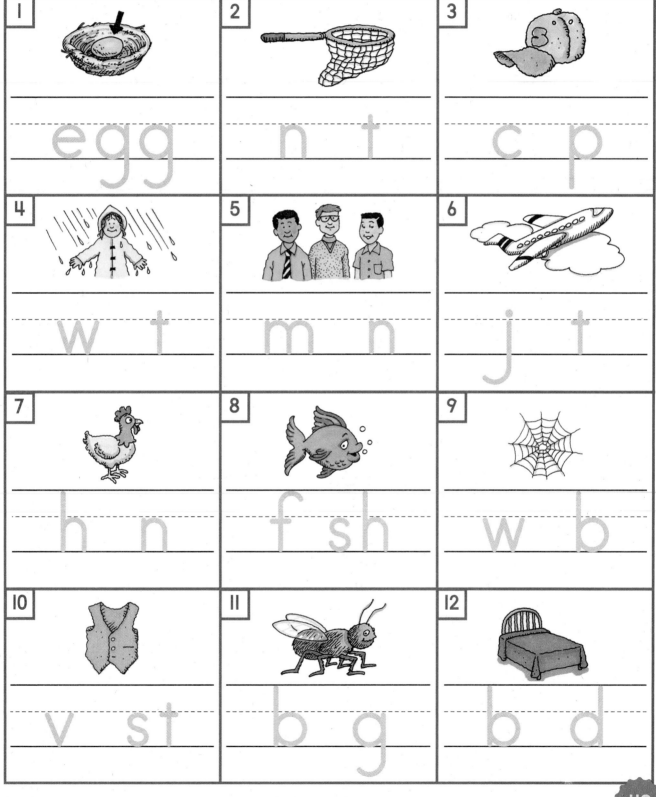

1	2	3
e g g	n t	c p
4	5	6
w t	m n	j t
7	8	9
h n	f sh	w b
10	11	12
v st	b g	b d

Short Vowel: / e /e   **113**

Name _____

1. hen

2.

3.

4.

5.

6.

7.

8.

9.

Short Vowel: / e / e • Writing Words with Short e   Phonics Practice Book

Harcourt Brace School Publishers

Name _____

The picture names in each row rhyme. Write the rhyming words.

1

j<u>et</u>

2

p<u>en</u>

Name _____

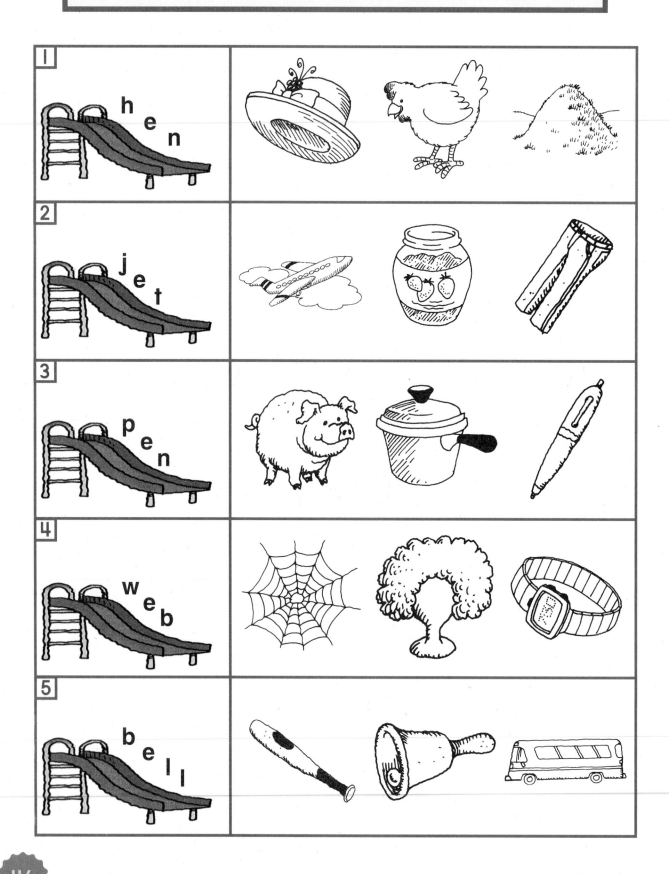

1. h e n

2. j e t

3. p e n

4. w e b

5. b e l l

Name _____

Write **e** to complete each word. Trace the whole word.
Then draw a picture for the word.

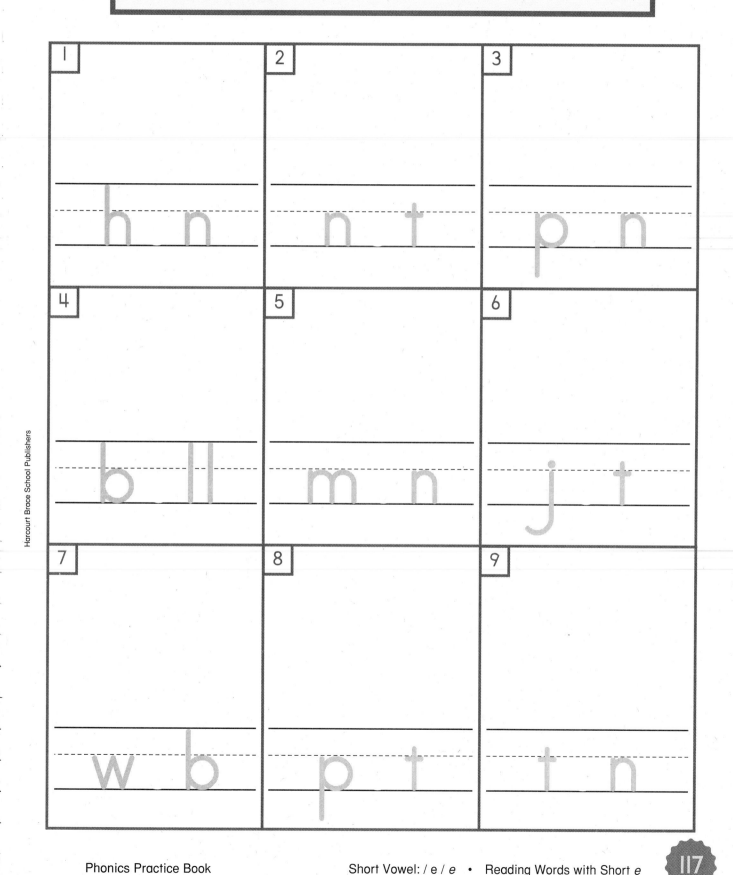

1 h _ n

2 n _ t

3 p _ n

4 b _ ll

5 m _ n

6 j _ t

7 w _ b

8 p _ t

9 t _ n

Harcourt Brace School Publishers

Name _____

Look at each picture. Write the word from the box that completes the sentence.

| hen | met | wet | jet | men | get |

1. She will _____ in.

2. The _____ can fly high.

3. The _____ will go in.

4. But she will be _____ .

5. The _____ look happy.

6. Have you _____ Ben?

Harcourt Brace School Publishers

Short Vowel: / e / e • Reading Words with Short e

Phonics Practice Book

Name _____

Circle the sentence that tells about each picture.

1.
Ken will see the hen.
Ken will not get wet.
Ken walks with the men.

2.
My pet likes the vet.
The vet jumps in the net.
The vet will let me ride.

3.
My pet is in a web.
My pet fell down.
A bell is on her neck.

4.
Get the hen out of the well.
Set the pen down.
Let Ben see the hen.

5.
The hen will get wet.
I bet you have a net.
Tell me why you fell.

6.
Nell met the vet.
Nell will sell the jet.
Nell will get a pet.

Name _____

A Girl and a Hen

Jen is my pet hen. We are friends.  We went on a boat ride. She fell out and got wet. Then we went to the vet. The vet said Jen can't get wet. If she gets wet, she can't lift her neck to peck.

I'm happy to have Jen back. Now I will not let her get wet.

1. What happened on the boat ride?

_____

_____

2. How does the girl feel about her pet? How do you know?

_____

_____

Now circle the story words that have the sound you hear in the middle of **bell.**

Short Vowel: / e / e • Reading Words in Context   Phonics Practice Book

Say the names of the pictures in each row. Color the pictures whose names rhyme.

Short Vowel: / i / • Phonemic Awareness

Name _____

Circle and color the pictures whose names have the
sound you hear in the middle of 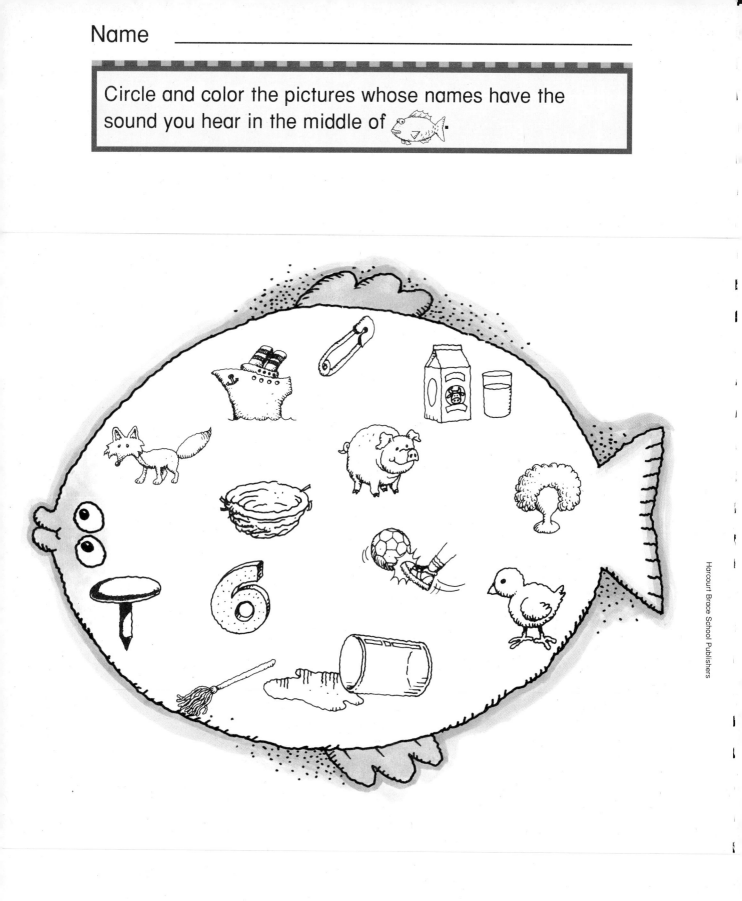.

Harcourt Brace School Publishers

Short Vowel: / i / • Phonemic Awareness

Phonics Practice Book

Name _____

Write **i** to complete each picture name that has the sound you hear in the middle of **fish.** Then trace the whole word.

f**i**sh

1	2	3
p i g	s __ t	l __ g
4	5	6
h __ l l	b __ d	b __ b
7	8	9
l __ d	s __ ck	h __ t
10	11	12
n __ t	p __ n	s __ x

Name _____

Write the name of each picture.

1. pig

2.

3.

4.

5.

6.

Short Vowel: / i / *i* • Writing Words with Short *i*

Phonics Practice Book

Harcourt Brace School Publishers

Name _____

The picture names in each row rhyme. Write the rhyming words.

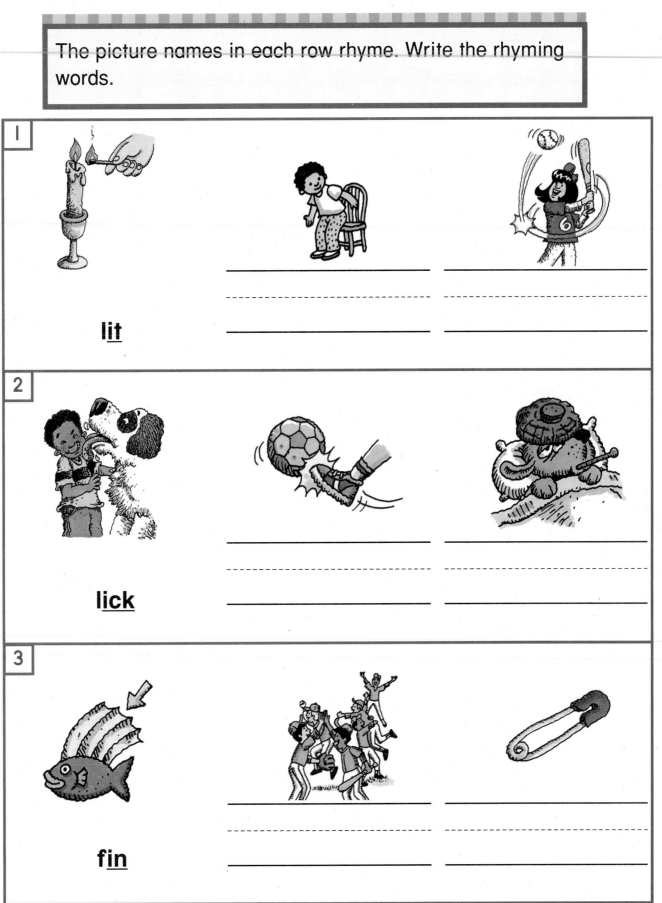

1
lit

2
lick

3
fin

Name _____

Slide and read each word. Color the picture it names.

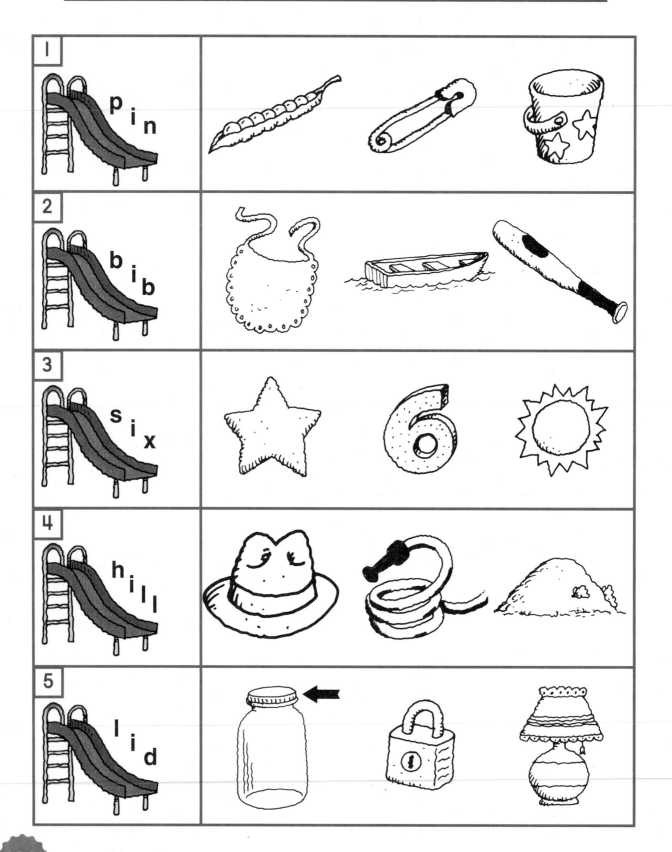

1	p i n			
2	b i b			
3	s i x			
4	h i l l			
5	l i d			

Short Vowel: / i / i • Blending

Phonics Practice Book

Name _____

Write **i** to complete each word. Trace the whole word.
Then draw a picture for the **word**.

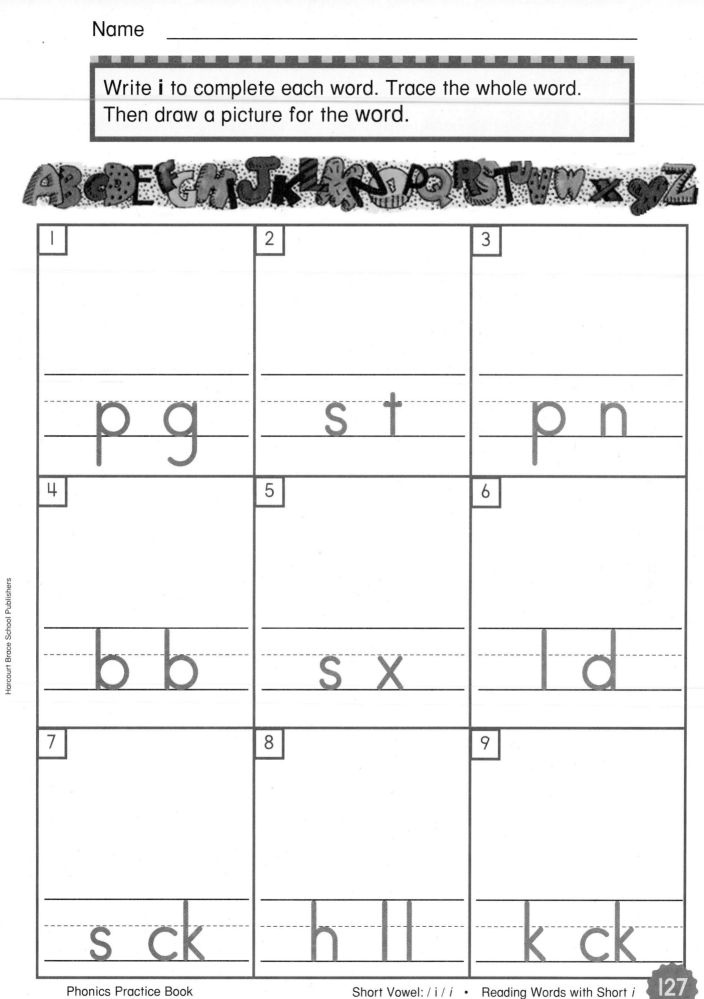

1	2	3
p g	s t	p n
4	5	6
b b	s x	l d
7	8	9
s ck	h ll	k ck

Phonics Practice Book   Short Vowel: / i / i • Reading Words with Short i   127

Harcourt Brace School Publishers

Name _____

Look at each picture. Write the word that completes the sentence.

hid   sip   hit   fit   brick   drip

1
_____
Jim will have a _____.

2
_____
He will fix it with a _____.

3
_____
My dog Zip _____.

4
_____
Zip will not _____.

5
_____
Will Jill get a _____?

6
_____
She's letting it _____.

Short Vowel: / i / i

Harcourt Brace School Publishers

Phonics Practice Book

Circle the sentence that tells about each picture.

1	The big dog jumps. The big dog sits. It is in a boat.
2	Now we win! Here is the pig! We can mix a cake.
3	Go up the hill. Put this in the van. Fill up the pan.
4	The lid is on the pot. She is in the garden. She did not have a bib.
5	Tim will go down the hill. Tim will go on a trip. Tim will put on a wig.
6	Did you fix it? Did you sit with me? Did you see all six?

Name _____

1. Look for the hill. Color it green.
2. Did you see the big pin? Circle it.
3. One dog can sit. Color this one.
4. Look for the bib. Color it blue.
5. Bill will dig. Do you see him? Color Bill.

Short Vowel: / i / i • Reading Words in Context

Phonics Practice Book

Name _____

Write **e** or **i** to complete each picture name. Then trace the whole word.

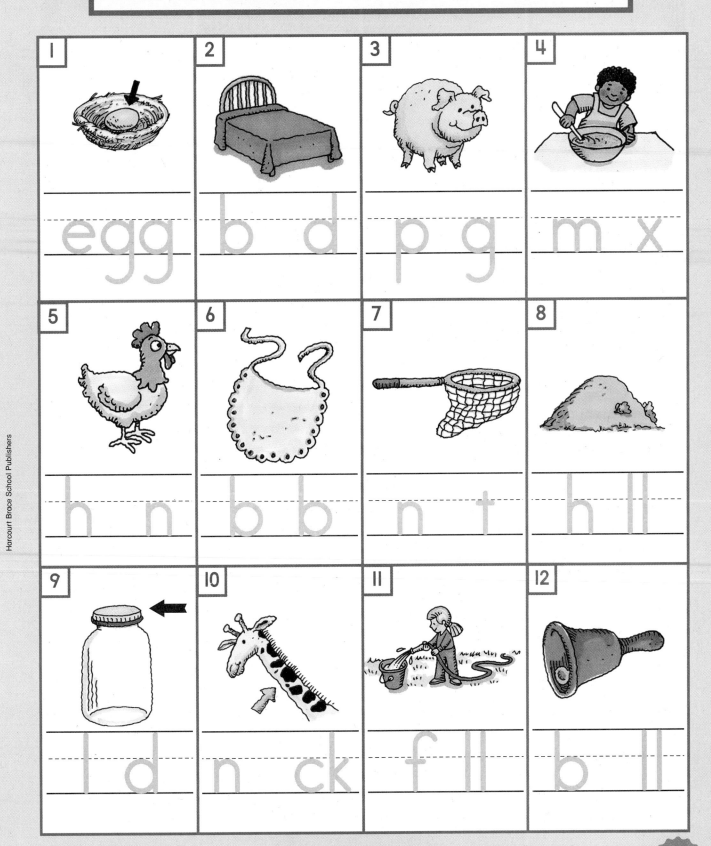

1. _____ egg

2. b _____ d

3. p _____ g

4. m _____ x

5. h _____ n

6. b _____ b

7. n _____ t

8. h _____ ll

9. l _____ d

10. n _____ ck

11. f _____ ll

12. b _____ ll

Name _____

Look at the pictures. Draw a line from each sentence to the picture it tells about.

1

It is a big hen.

This is my bed.

I will sit here.

2

Ken sees a jet.

Ted sees a pin.

Bill sees a hill.

3

This fish is a pet.

This fish is in a net.

Six big fish jump.

4

The men will get it.

Yes, he hit it!

Will he kick it?

Say the names of the pictures in each row. Color the pictures whose names rhyme.

Short Vowel: / u / • Phonemic Awareness

Name _____

Say the name of each picture. Color the pictures whose names have the sound you hear in the middle of 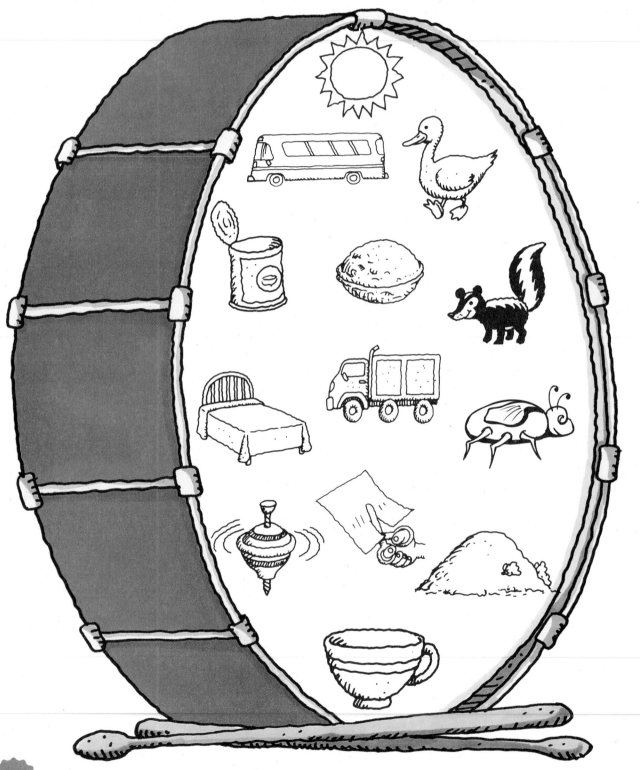 .

Short Vowel: / u / • Phonemic Awareness

Phonics Practice Book

Name _____

Write **u** to complete each picture name that has the sound you hear in the middle of **sun**. Then trace the whole word.

s<u>u</u>n

1. sun

2. d _ ck

3. t _ n

4. t _ b

5. p _ g

6. b _ s

7. m _ p

8. c _ b

9. n _ t

10. c _ p

11. b _ g

12. s _ b

Name _____

Write the name of each picture.

1
jug

2

3

4

5

6

7

8

9

Harcourt Brace School Publishers

The picture names in each row rhyme. Write the rhyming words.

1. fun

2. sum

3. tub

Name _____

Slide and read each word. Color the picture it names.

1. s u n

2. b u s

3. c u p

4. h u g

5. d r u m

Short Vowel: / u / u • Blending

Harcourt Brace School Publishers

Phonics Practice Book

Name _____

Write **u** to complete each word. Then trace the whole word. Draw a picture for the word.

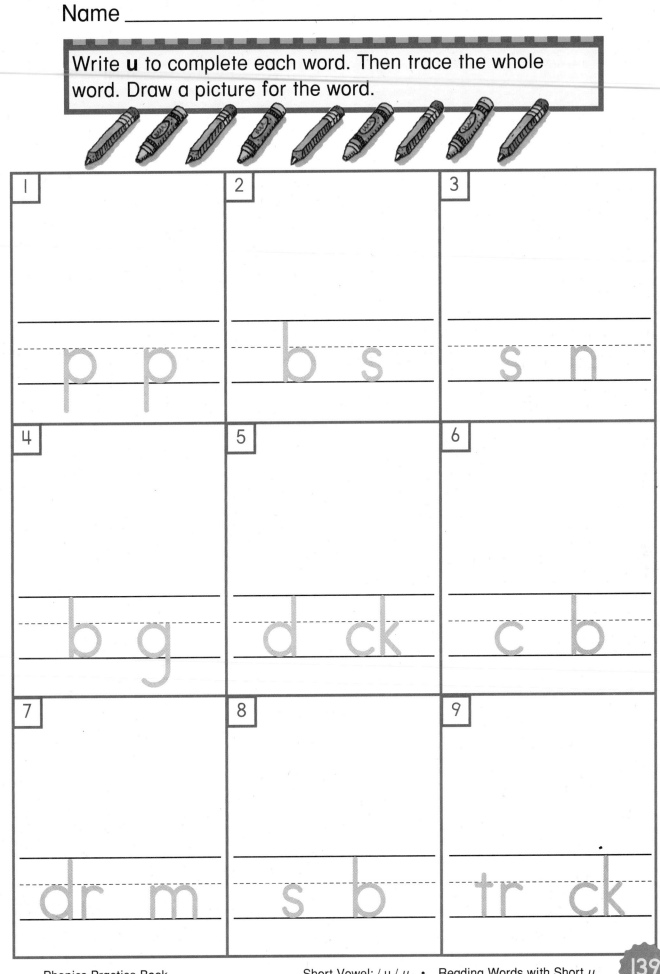

1	2	3
p___p	b___s	s___n

4	5	6
b___g	d___ck	c___b

7	8	9
dr___m	s___b	tr___ck

Name _____

Look at each picture. Write the word from the box that completes the sentence.

rug	mud	tug
bus	bun	fun

1. The hot dog comes on

_____

a _____.

2.

_____

We can't play in the _____.

3.

_____

So we play on the _____.

4.

_____

We all have to _____!

5.

_____

We can always have _____.

6.

_____

We get on the _____.

Short Vowel: / u / u • Reading Words with Short u

Phonics Practice Book

Name _____

Read the poem. Then write a word from the poem to complete each sentence.

A Duck and His Quack

Chuck, a duck, was out of luck.
He could not quack. He could only cluck.
He went to his friend, Bub, a grub.
Bub let Chuck scrub in his big tub.
The bath did not help Chuck too much.
He wanted his quack back, and such.
He was sad and glum—but then
He bumped heads with Glenn the hen.
Now Chuck could quack just like a duck.
And Glenn, the hen, well, she could cluck.

1. Chuck could only

_____

_____.

_____
----

2. Bub is a _____.

_____
----

3. Chuck _____ heads with Glenn.

Name _____

Do what the sentences tell you.

1. Do you see the sun? Color it.

2. Look for the truck. Color it blue.

3. Now find the bus. Color it too.

4. Find the ducks. Circle the duck with the drum.

5. Draw a bug on the jug.

6. Find the pups. Draw a pup in the mud.

Now circle the words that have the sound you hear in the middle of **sun**.

Name _____

Write **a, e, i, o**, or **u** to complete each picture name. Then trace the whole word.

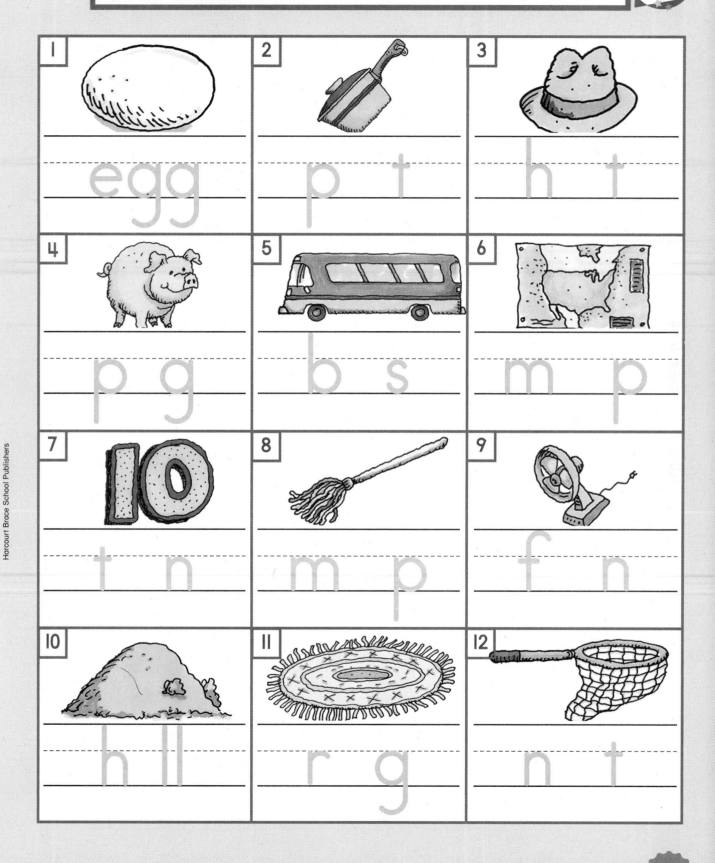

1. egg

2. p ___ t

3. h ___ t

4. p ___ g

5. b ___ s

6. m ___ p

7. t ___ n

8. m ___ p

9. f ___ n

10. h ___ ll

11. r ___ g

12. n ___ t

Name _____

Circle the sentence that tells about each picture.

1. Jack will get the net.

   Bill can fit in the bus.

   Tom can hop and run.

2. Kim picks up the cup.

   Dot hit it with the bat.

   Pam sat on the hill.

3. This pig will fix the fan.

   The pig digs in the mud.

   A pig gets wet in the well.

4. The fox sees ten big hens.

   The duck sits with the bug.

   The fox will not get in the bag.

5. The cub naps in his bed.

   The bed is on a red rug.

   The cub runs to the top.

Harcourt Brace School Publishers

Name _____

1

○ hat
○ hot
○ hut

2

○ pan
○ pond
○ pin

3

○ cab
○ cub
○ cob

4

○ pet
○ pit
○ pot

5

○ nut
○ not
○ net

6

○ big
○ bug
○ bag

7

○ sack
○ sock
○ sick

8

○ hit
○ hot
○ hat

9

○ tin
○ ten
○ tan

10

○ cut
○ cot
○ cat

11

○ deck
○ dock
○ duck

12

○ bed
○ bad
○ bud

Name _____

Fill in the circle next to the sentence that tells about the picture.

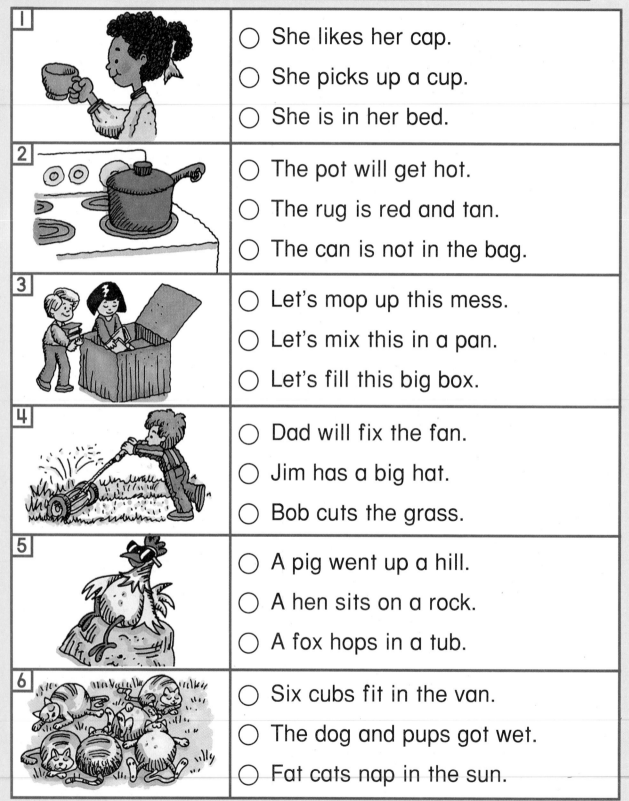

1.
- ○ She likes her cap.
- ○ She picks up a cup.
- ○ She is in her bed.

2.
- ○ The pot will get hot.
- ○ The rug is red and tan.
- ○ The can is not in the bag.

3.
- ○ Let's mop up this mess.
- ○ Let's mix this in a pan.
- ○ Let's fill this big box.

4.
- ○ Dad will fix the fan.
- ○ Jim has a big hat.
- ○ Bob cuts the grass.

5.
- ○ A pig went up a hill.
- ○ A hen sits on a rock.
- ○ A fox hops in a tub.

6.
- ○ Six cubs fit in the van.
- ○ The dog and pups got wet.
- ○ Fat cats nap in the sun.

Harcourt Brace School Publishers

Write **ea** under each picture whose name has the sound you hear in the middle of **thread**. Then trace the whole word.

thread

1 br___d

2 t___ck

3 h___d

4 thr___d

5 f___sh

6 h___vy

Short Vowel: / e / *ea* /

Name _____

Look at each picture. Circle the word that completes the sentence. Then write the word.

1	Put this on your _____ _____ .	hill head had
2	_____ _____ , set, go!	Rock Ready Rip
3	We are out of _____ _____ .	brand bring breath
4	Here is the _____ _____ .	bread brick brag
5	_____ I will _____ it for you.	spot spring spread

Harcourt Brace School Publishers

Name _____

Say the names of the pictures in each row. Color the pictures whose names rhyme.

Harcourt Brace School Publishers

Help the 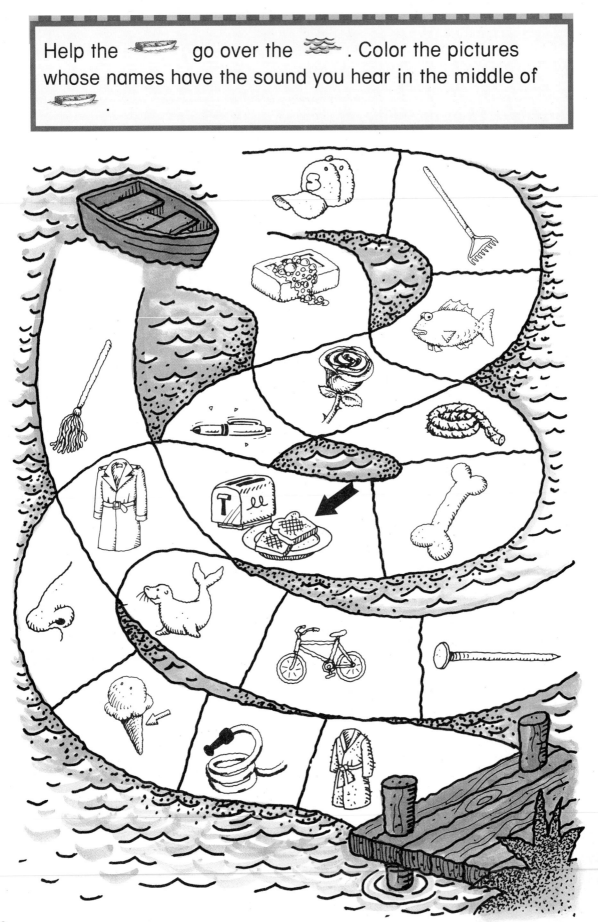 go over the 〰〰. Color the pictures whose names have the sound you hear in the middle of ⌐⌐ .

Long Vowel: /ō/ • Phonemic Awareness

Phonics Practice Book

Harcourt Brace School Publishers

Name _____

The picture names in each row rhyme. Write the rhyming words.

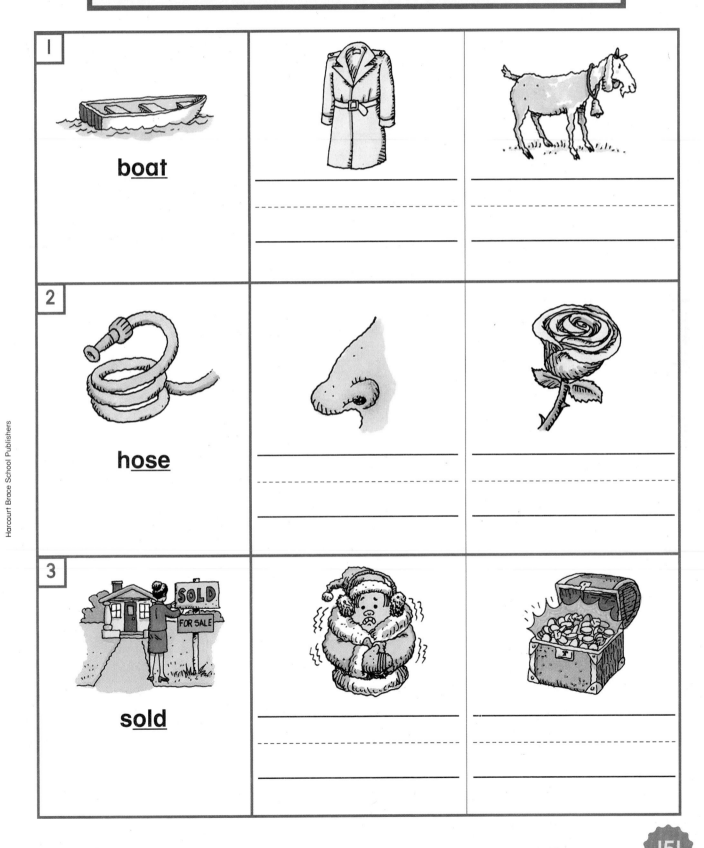

b<u>oat</u>

h<u>ose</u>

s<u>old</u>

Harcourt Brace School Publishers

Name _____

Rope has the long **o** sound. Write **o** in the middle and **e** at the end of each word that has the long **o** sound. Then trace the whole word.

r**o**p**e**

1 r p

2 b n

3 c g

4 p l

5 d g

6 r s

7 f v

8 r b

9 c n

10 n s

11 c p

12 h l

Name _____

Boat has the long **o** sound. Write **oa** to complete each word that has the long **o** sound. Then trace the whole word.

b**oa**t

1	2	3
boat	s____p	__c__t

4	5	6
j____p	t____d	g____t

7	8	9
c____t	b____x	r____d

Name _____

Old has the long **o** sound. Write **o** to complete each word that has the long **o** sound. Then trace the whole word.

old

1	2	3
old	pple	c ld
4	5	6
n	f ld	f x
7	8	9
k te	s ld	g ld

Long Vowel: / ō / o, oa, o-e

Harcourt Brace School Publishers

Phonics Practice Book

The **o-e** in **rope**, the **oa** in **boat**, and the **o** in **old** all stand for the long **o** sound. Write the words where they belong on the lists. Then draw a picture for the last word you write in each list.

go   rose   coat
toad   toast   home
bone   cold   gold

1. r<u>o</u>p<u>e</u>

2. b<u>oa</u>t

3. <u>o</u>ld

Name _____

Slide and read each word. Color the picture it names.

1. b o a t

2. r o b e

3. c o a t

4. h o s e

5. c o n e

Long Vowel: / ō / *o, oa, o-e* • Blending

Harcourt Brace School Publishers

Phonics Practice Book

Name _____

Circle the name of each picture. Then write the words.

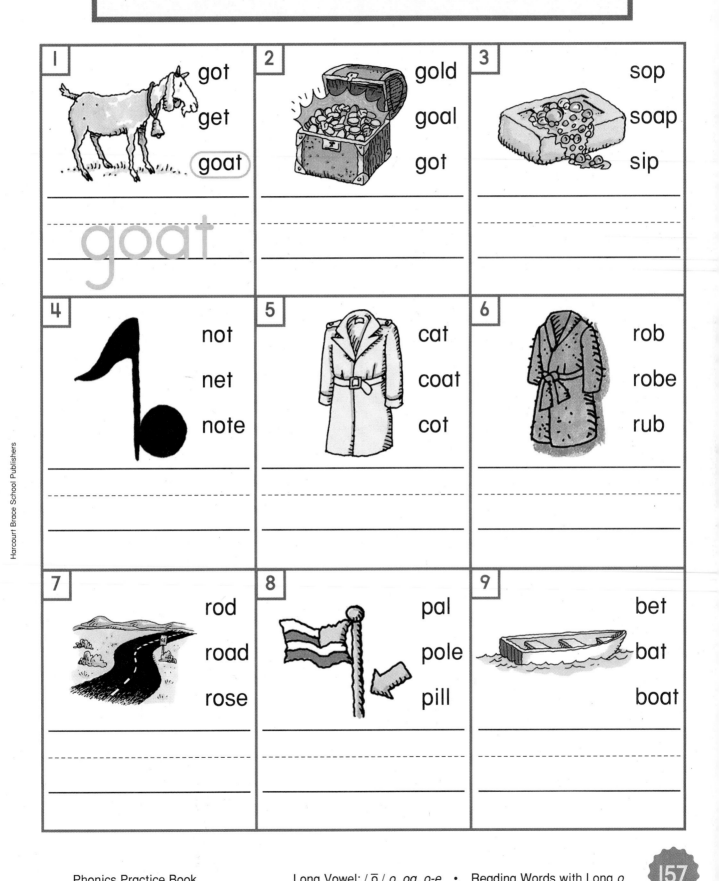

1. got / get / (goat)

goat

2. gold / goal / got

3. sop / soap / sip

4. not / net / note

5. cat / coat / cot

6. rob / robe / rub

7. rod / road / rose

8. pal / pole / pill

9. bet / bat / boat

Harcourt Brace School Publishers

Phonics Practice Book

Long Vowel: / ō / o, oa, o-e • Reading Words with Long o

157

Name _____

Say the name of each picture. Circle the words in the box that rhyme with the picture's name.

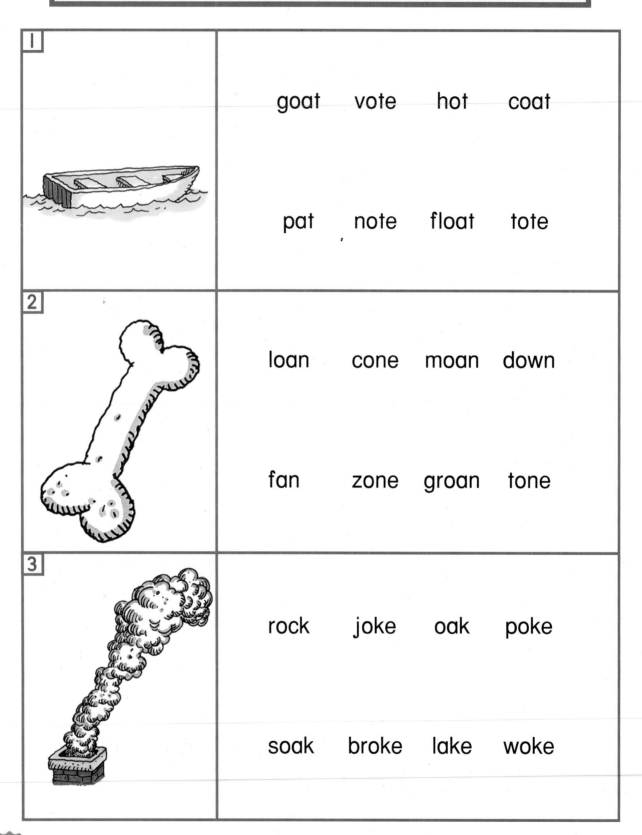

1

| goat | vote | hot | coat |
| pat | note | float | tote |

2

| loan | cone | moan | down |
| fan | zone | groan | tone |

3

| rock | joke | oak | poke |
| soak | broke | lake | woke |

Harcourt Brace School Publishers

Long Vowel: / ō / o, oa, o-e • Reading Words with Long o   Phonics Practice Book

Name _____

Write the word that completes each sentence.

| hose | bone | told |
| soap | hope | hole |

1. I have a big _____ .

2. I will put it in this _____ .

3. Joan went to get some _____ .

4. Water comes out of the _____ .

5. I _____ she does not see me.

6. She _____ me not to dig.

Harcourt Brace School Publishers

Name _____

Circle and write the word that completes each sentence.

1		_____ "Let's _____ for a ride!"	goat get go
2		_____ We _____ for a long time.	drip drove dock
3		We went to an _____ _____ garden.	only off old
4		_____ We saw a _____ jump away.	goat goal got
5		I climbed a big _____ _____ tree.	toad oak only

Long Vowel: / ō / o, oa, o-e • Reading Words with Long o

Phonics Practice Book

Name _____

Say the names of the pictures in each row. Color the pictures whose names rhyme.

Long Vowel: /ī/ • Phonemic Awareness

Name _____

Color the pictures whose names have the sound you hear in the middle of 9 .

Draw three things whose names have the sound you hear in the middle of 9 .

Long Vowel: / ī / • Phonemic Awareness

Phonics Practice Book

The picture names in each row rhyme. Write the rhyming words.

1 tight

2 p<u>ine</u>

3 <u>slide</u>

Long Vowel: /ī/ *i, igh, i-e* • Phonograms

Name _____

Harcourt Brace School Publishers

Nine has the long **i** sound. Write **i** in the middle and **e** at the end of each word that has the long **i** sound. Then trace the whole word.

nine

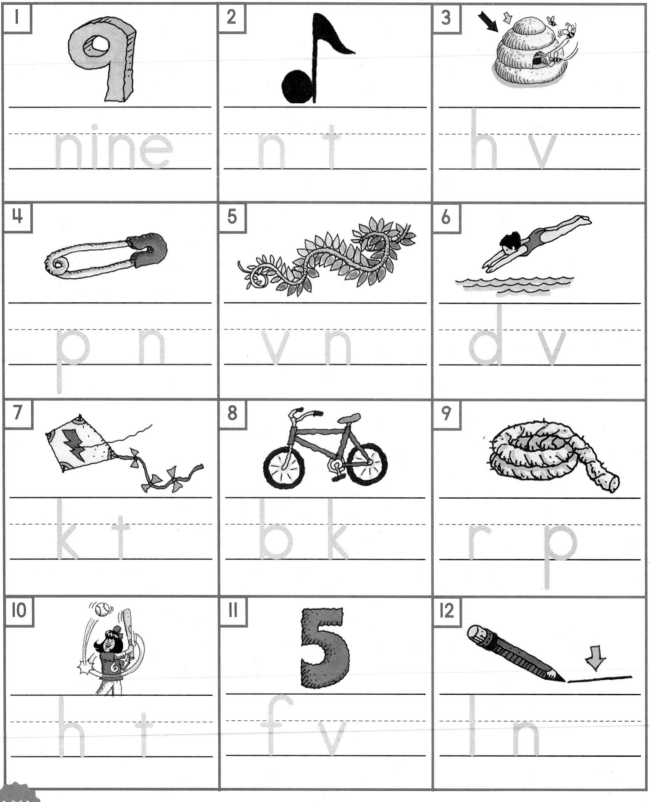

Long Vowel: / ī / i, igh, i-e

Phonics Practice Book

Name _____

hi

knight

The **i** in **hi** and the **igh** in **knight** both stand for the long **i** sound. Write the word that completes each sentence.

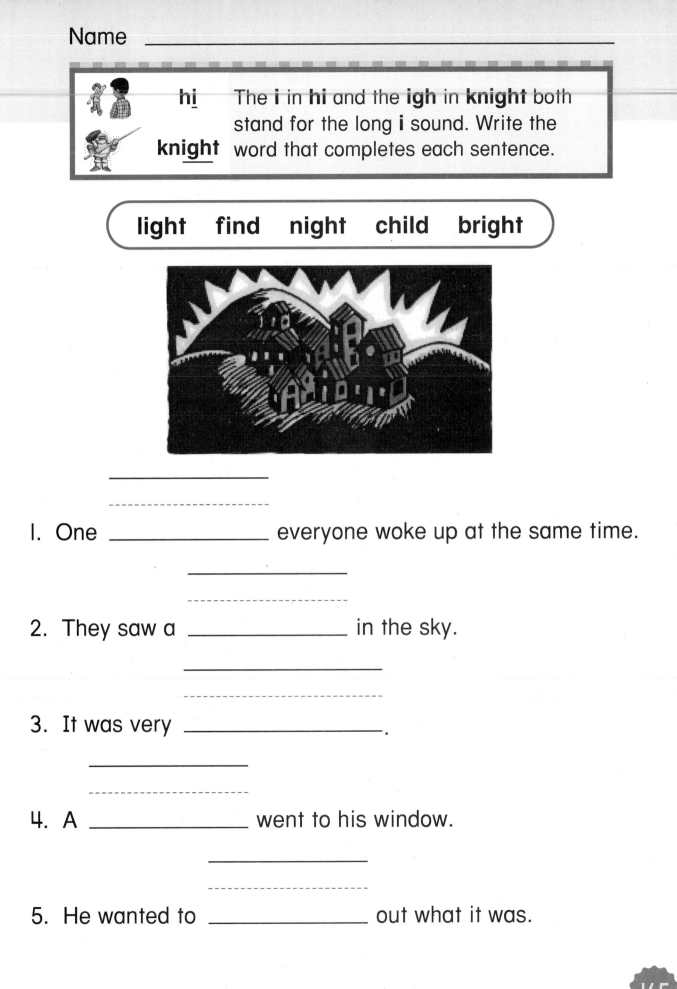

| light | find | night | child | bright |

_____
- - - - - - - - - - - - - - -

1. One _____ everyone woke up at the same time.

_____
- - - - - - - - - - - - - - -

2. They saw a _____ in the sky.

_____
- - - - - - - - - - - - - - -

3. It was very _____.

_____
- - - - - - - - - - - - - - -

4. A _____ went to his window.

_____
- - - - - - - - - - - - - - -

5. He wanted to _____ out what it was.

Name _____

The **i–e** in **nine,** the **i** in **hi,** and the **igh** in **knight** all stand for the long **i** sound. Write the words where they belong on the lists. Then draw a picture for the last word on each list.

tight   kite   wild   drive
find   night   child   light   bike

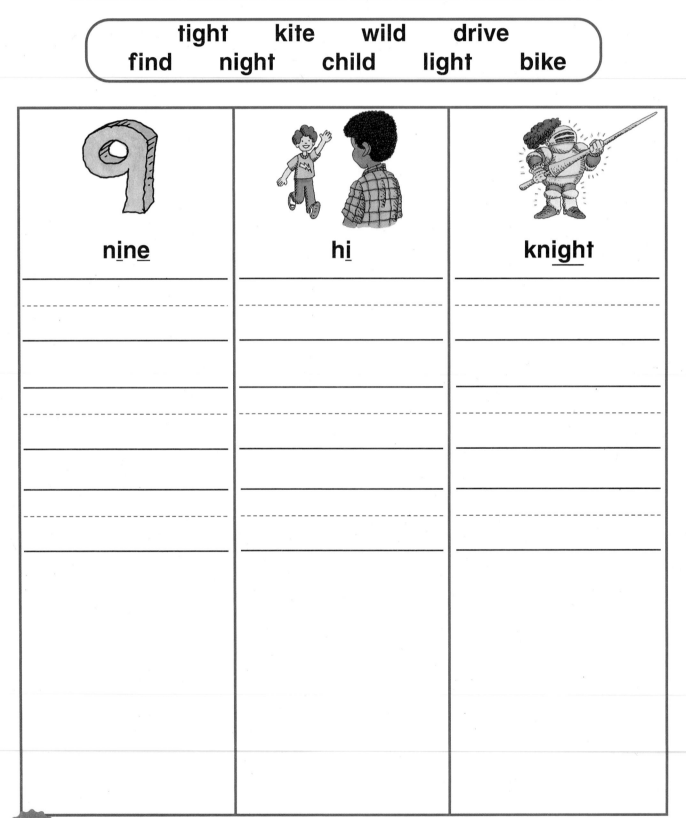

nine _____

hi _____

knight _____

Long Vowel /ī/ *i, igh, i-e* • Sorting Words with Long *i*

Phonics Practice Book

Harcourt Brace School Publishers

Slide and read each word. Color the picture it names.

Long Vowel: /ī/ i, igh, i-e • Blending

Name _____

Circle the name of each picture. Then write the word.

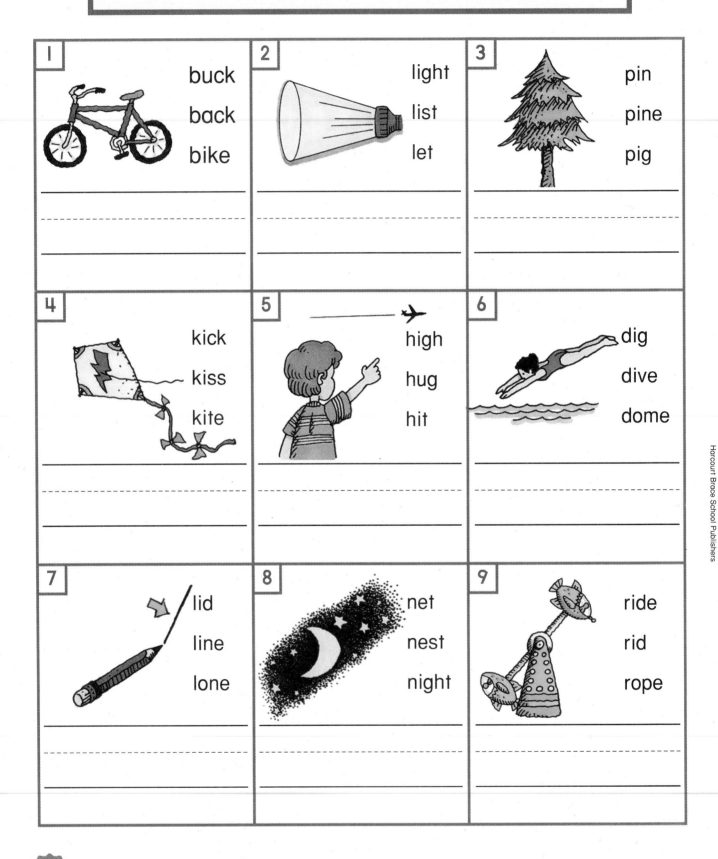

1.
buck
back
bike

2.
light
list
let

3.
pin
pine
pig

4.
kick
kiss
kite

5.
high
hug
hit

6.
dig
dive
dome

7.
lid
line
lone

8.
net
nest
night

9.
ride
rid
rope

Harcourt Brace School Publishers

Say the name of each picture. Circle the words in the box that rhyme with the picture name.

1	light bite note might right tight sit white
2	fine cane line mine pin pine shine vine
7	ride hide side lid pride wide code glide

Name _____

Ranger Pike's Find

Ranger Pike hiked into the hills to find

Five baby bats that were on her mind.

The sun went down, and soon it was night.

Ranger Pike climbed a vine and shined her light.

She saw the five bats rise into her sight.

She smiled as she walked down the hill that night

Because all five bats were quite all right.

1. Why did Ranger Pike walk into the hills?

_____

- -

_____

2. Why did Ranger Pike smile?

_____

- -

_____

- -

_____

Name _____

Do what the sentences tell you.

1. Mr. Miles rides a bike. Circle Mr. Miles and his bike.

2. What is a mile high in the sky? Color it.

3. Do you see a kite? Color it bright green.

4. One plant grows high. Draw one more just like it.

5. Swipe the cat likes to hide in the garden. Draw a line under Swipe.

6. Find the light that will shine at night. Draw a box around it.

Now circle the words that have the long **i** sound.

Name _____

Write the word that completes each sentence.

| fine | fight | wild | bite | kind | night |

1. My cat Spike _____

   is a little bit _____ .

2. We can't _____

   let him out at _____ .

3. If we do, _____

   he gets into a _____ .

4. One time, he got a _____

   bad _____ on his side.

5. The vet was _____

   very _____ to him.

6. After a while, _____

   Spike was just _____ .

Long Vowel: / ī / i, igh, i-e • Reading Words with Long i

Name _____

Write the word that names each picture.

kite	hose	road	night	rope	nine
note	gold	find	hi	light	boat

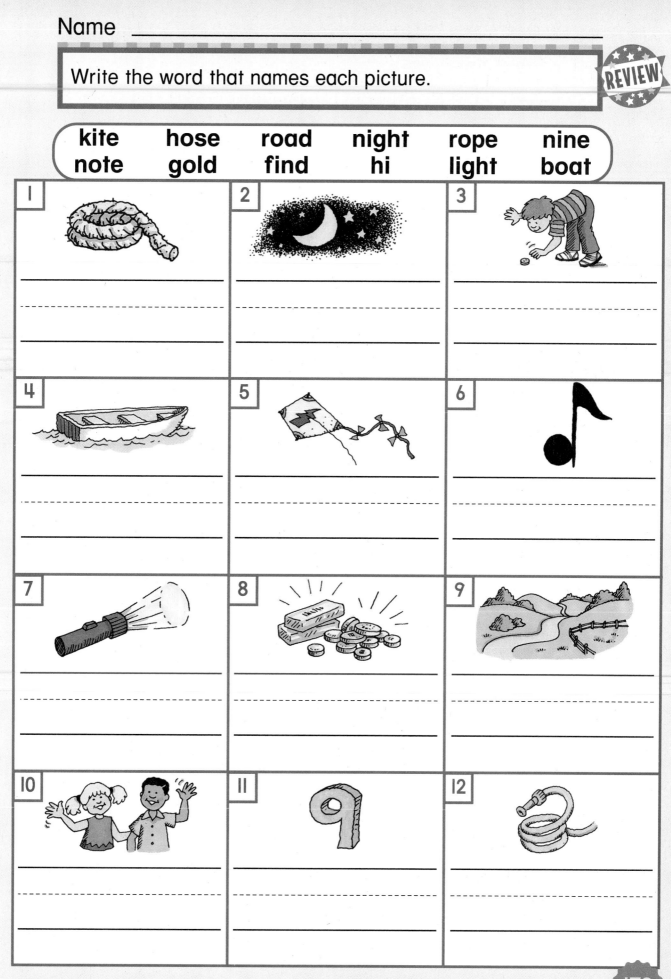

1.

2.

3.

4.

5.

6.

7.

8.

9.

10.

11.

12.

Review of Long Vowels: / ō / o, oa, o-e; / ī /i, igh, i-e

Name _____

Circle and write the word that completes each sentence.

1	_____ ---------------------- This is the _____ to take.	rod road ride
2	_____ ---------------------- Mr. Jiles lives a _____ up the hill.	mile must mint
3	_____ ---------------------- We like his _____ house.	old over no
4	_____ ---------------------- At _____ you can see the lights of the town.	nose night no
5	_____ ---------------------- We bring a _____ for his dog, Coach.	bright boat bone
6	We think Mr. Jiles couldn't _____ ---------------------- _____ a better home.	fish find fold

Review of Long Vowels: / ō / o, oa, o-e; / ī / i, igh, i-e

Phonics Practice Book

Harcourt Brace School Publishers

Name _____

Say the names of the pictures in each row. Color the
pictures whose names rhyme.

Name _____

Help the  get to the . Color the pictures whose names have the sound you hear in the middle of and at the end of .

Long Vowel: /ē/ • Phonemic Awareness

Phonics Practice Book

Harcourt Brace School Publishers

Name _____

The picture names in each row rhyme. Write the rhyming words.

1

steam

2

wheel

3

knee

Name _____

bead

Bead has the long **e** sound. Write **ea** to complete each word that has the long **e** sound. Then trace the whole word.

1	2	3
b ___ k	p ___ s	s ___ p
4 10	**5**	**6**
t ___ n	s ___ l	l ___ f
7	**8**	**9**
p ___ p	ch ___ t	h ___ t
10	**11**	**12**
j ___ ns	n ___ t	t ___ m

178

Long Vowel: / ē / e, ea, ee

Phonics Practice Book

Harcourt Brace School Publishers

Name _____

wh__ee__l

Wheel has the long **e** sound. Write **ee** to complete each word that has the long **e** sound. Then trace the whole word.

1	2	3
_____ wh _____ l	_____ g _____ t	_____ b _____
4	5	6
_____ j _____ p	_____ s _____ d	_____ m _____ p
7	8	9
_____ m _____ n	_____ tr _____	_____ sh _____ p
10	11	12
_____ thr _____	_____ t _____ d	_____ f _____ t

Long Vowel: / ē /e, ea, ee

179

Name _____

me

The word **me** has the long **e** sound. Write the word that completes each sentence.

be she he we me

1 I think _____ will catch it.

2 I think _____ will find me.

3 Let _____ have a turn.

4 We will _____ in trouble!

5 What can _____ do?

Long Vowel: / ē / e, ea, ee • Reading Words with Long e   Phonics Practice Book

The **ea** in **bead**, the **ee** in **wheel**, and the **e** in **me** all stand for the long **e** sound. Write the words where they belong on the lists. Then draw a picture for the last word on each list.

he	leaf	tree	beach	she
feet	dream	bee	we

bead	**wheel**	**me**

Name _____

Slide and read each word. Color the picture it names.

Long Vowel: / ē / e, ea, ee • Blending

Phonics Practice Book

Harcourt Brace School Publishers

Name _____

Circle the name of each picture. Then write the word.

1.
bed
boat
(bead)

bead

2.
seed
side
sad

3.
beak
bike
beam

4.
pill
peas
peel

5.
be
he
she

6.
meal
mole
me

7.
shop
sheep
ship

8.
fast
fight
feet

9.
road
read
ride

Name _____

| 1 | meet   heat   feet   boat |
| | neat   pet   treat   sheet |

| 2 | bee   hi   we   tea |
| | go   tree   see   me |

| 3 | real   feel   tell   seal |
| | heel   deal   goal   peel |

Long Vowel: /ē/ e, ea, ee • Reading Words with Long e

Name _____

tree   eat   seed   beak   be   feed

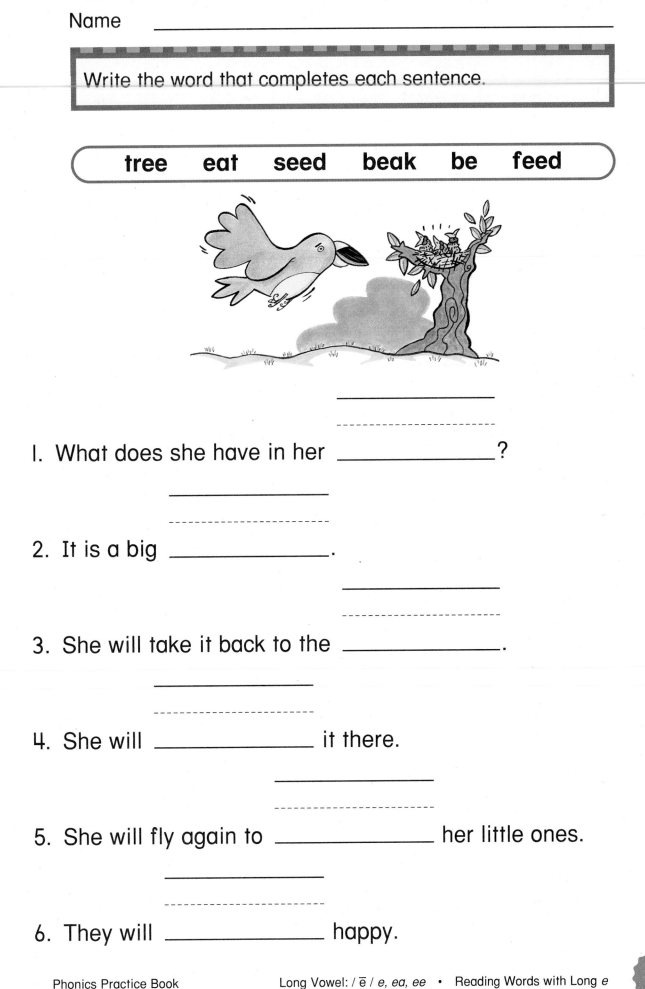

_____

- - - - - - - - - - - - - - - - -

1. What does she have in her _____?

_____

- - - - - - - - - - - - - - - - -

2. It is a big _____.

_____

- - - - - - - - - - - - - - - - -

3. She will take it back to the _____.

_____

- - - - - - - - - - - - - - - - -

4. She will _____ it there.

_____

- - - - - - - - - - - - - - - - -

5. She will fly again to _____ her little ones.

_____

- - - - - - - - - - - - - - - - -

6. They will _____ happy.

Name _____

A DAY AT THE BEACH

One day we went to the beach. We saw that the beach was not clean. Everybody put the trash in bags.

We had our sandwiches under a big tree. We ran and played after our meal. Jean shouted that she saw a seal. A bee almost bit Lee.

Soon it was time to leave. We had to make the beach clean and neat. We didn't want to go. Next week we will come back to this beach by the sea.

Why did they clean the beach?

_____
- -
_____
_____
- -
_____

Name _____

Say the names of the pictures in each row. Color the pictures whose names rhyme.

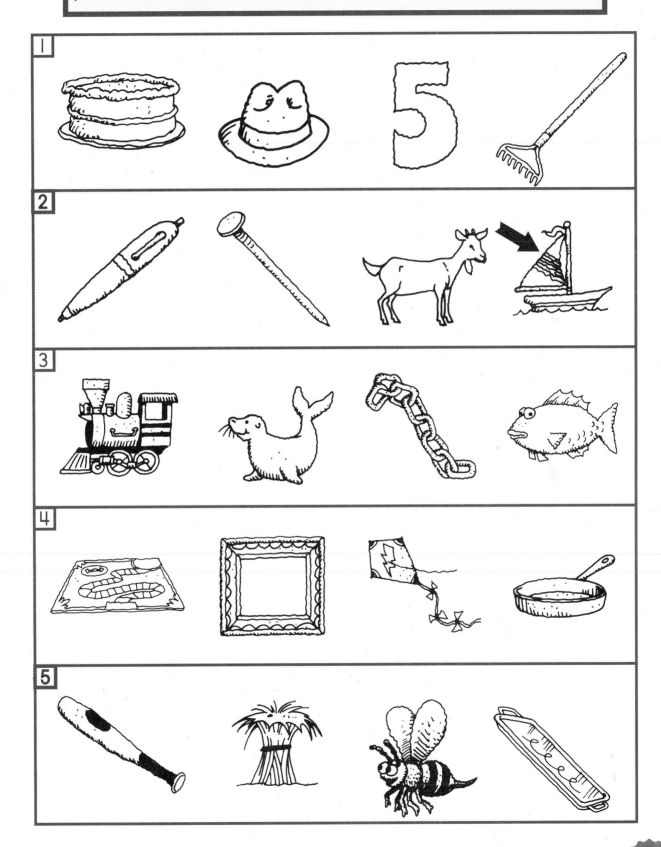

Help the  get out of the ⫻ . Color the pictures whose names have the sound you hear in the middle of 🐌 and ⫻ .

Name _____

The picture names in each row rhyme. Write the rhyming words.

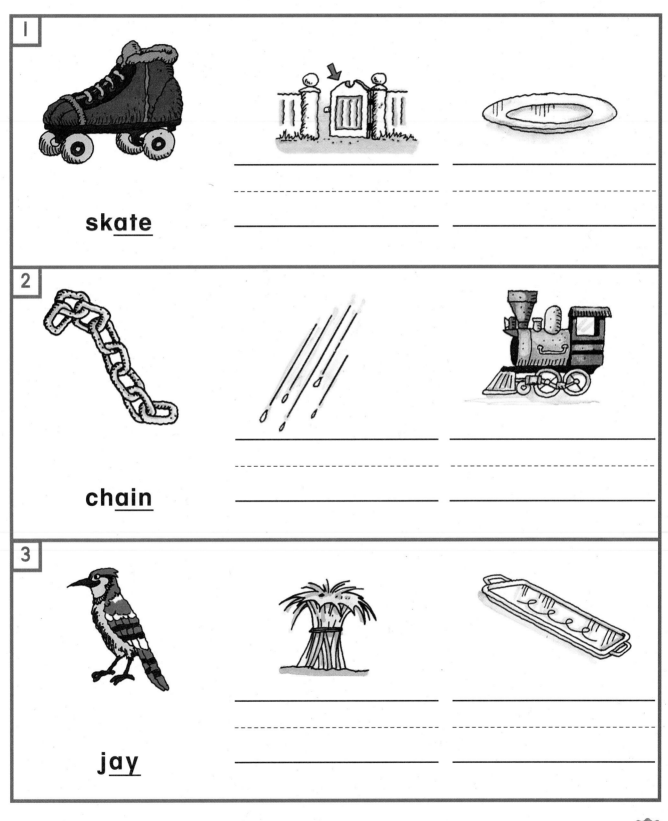

1

skate

_____

- - - - - - - - - - -

_____

_____

- - - - - - - - - - -

_____

2

chain

_____

- - - - - - - - - - -

_____

_____

- - - - - - - - - - -

_____

3

jay

_____

- - - - - - - - - - -

_____

_____

- - - - - - - - - - -

_____

Name _____

Mail has the long **a** sound. Write **ai** to complete each word that has the long **a** sound. Then trace the whole word.

mail

1	2	3
pail	b___t	___r___n

4	5	6
l___f	t___l	p___nt

7	8	9
n___l	j___p	tr___n

Harcourt Brace School Publishers

Name _____

jay

Jay has the long **a** sound. Write **ay** to complete each word that has the long **a** sound. Then trace the whole word.

1	2	3
jay	d___	b___
4	5	6
h___	p___	tr___
7	8	9
tr___	p___	pl___

Long Vowel: / ā / ai, ay, a-e

Name _____

gate

Gate has the long **a** sound. Write **a** in the middle and **e** at the end of each word that has the long **a** sound. Then trace the whole word.

1	2	3
w v	t p	n n
4	5	6
c n	wh l	g m
7	8	9
k t	r k	sk t
10	11	12
c g	b n	c k

Long Vowel: / ā / *ai, ay, a-e*

Phonics Practice Book

Name _____

The **ai** in **mail**, the **ay** in **jay**, and the **a-e** in **cane** all stand for the long **a** sound. Write the words where they belong on the lists. Then draw a picture for the last word in each list.

| hay | snail | grape | cake | tray | braid |
| day | game | rain | play | plate | train |

1 m<u>ai</u>l

2 j<u>ay</u>

3 c<u>a</u>n<u>e</u>

Name _____

Slide and read each word. Color the picture it names.

1. cake

2. tail

3. tray

4. pail

5. game

Long Vowel: / ā / *ai, ay, a-e* • Blending

Phonics Practice Book

Harcourt Brace School Publishers

Name _____

1. pan
   pole
   (pail)

   pail

2. gate
   game
   goat

3. hay
   hat
   hair

4. can
   cane
   cone

5. braid
   branch
   brick

6. rug
   ran
   rain

7. mail
   mile
   meal

8. snore
   sneak
   snake

9. snake
   say
   see

Name _____

Say the name of each picture. Circle the words that rhyme with the picture's name.

1	
	main Jane bone rain cane pan plane pain
2	
	may see day way play gray high say
3	
	sail whale pail pole tell mail scale trail

Long Vowel: / ā / ai, ay, a-e • Reading Words with Long a   Phonics Practice Book

Name _____

Circle the sentence that tells about each picture.

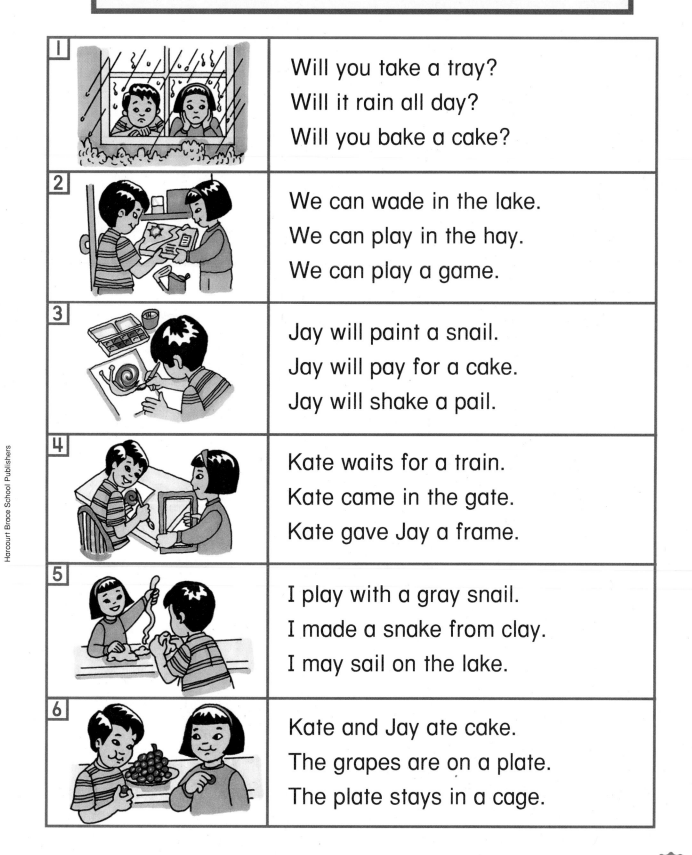

1. Will you take a tray?
   Will it rain all day?
   Will you bake a cake?

2. We can wade in the lake.
   We can play in the hay.
   We can play a game.

3. Jay will paint a snail.
   Jay will pay for a cake.
   Jay will shake a pail.

4. Kate waits for a train.
   Kate came in the gate.
   Kate gave Jay a frame.

5. I play with a gray snail.
   I made a snake from clay.
   I may sail on the lake.

6. Kate and Jay ate cake.
   The grapes are on a plate.
   The plate stays in a cage.

Name _____

Do what the sentences tell you. Then circle the words that have the long **a** sound.

1. Mr. Gray paints. Draw a pail of paint for him.

2. Do you see a tray? You may draw a cake on it.

3. Find Kate. She has braids. Put skates on her feet.

4. Find the frame. Inside it, draw a place where you play.

5. Find Jake. He likes to wave. Draw a cape on him.

6. Ms. May has paid for the grapes. Color Ms. May.

Long Vowel: / ā / ai, ay, a-e • Reading Words in Context   Phonics Practice Book

Name _____

REVIEW

cake leaf bee feet rain game read tray mail

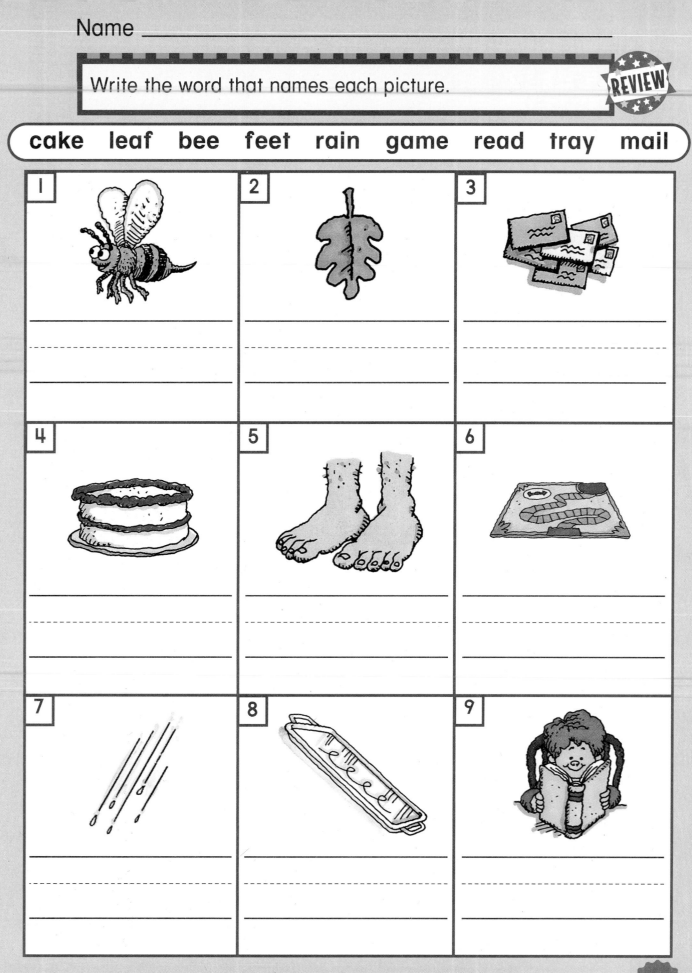

1

2

3

4

5

6

7

8

9

Review of Long Vowels: / ē / e, ee, ea; / ā / ai, ay, a-e

199

Name _____

Circle the word that completes each sentence. Then write the word.

1	We went to _____ ------------------ _____ the animals.	stop see say
2	Nate liked the _____ ------------------ _____ best.	snails seeds snakes
3	We watched the lions _____ ------------------ eat a _____.	meal map mail
4	We saw baby apes jump _____ ------------------ and _____.	paint play peel
5	Three seals ate fish _____ ------------------ from a _____.	pole pill pail

Review of Long Vowels: / ē / e, ee, ea; / ā / ai, ay, a-e   Phonics Practice Book

Name _____

Find the words in the puzzle. Circle them. Some words go across. Some words go down.

mule   cute   huge   cube

c	u	b	e	m
u	l	r	w	h
t	f	s	o	u
e	d	t	k	g
z	m	u	l	e

Now write the word that names each picture.

| 1 | 2 |
| 3 | 4 |

Long Vowel: / yōō / *u-e*

201

Name _____

| huge | use | cute |
| mule | use | cube |

_____
- -

1. The _____ is in the garden.

_____
- -

2. The boy will _____ his cap to chase it out.

_____
- -

3. The baby ducks are _____.

_____
- -

4. That baby duck thinks the horse is _____.

_____
- -

5. Mother puts an ice _____ in the water.

Long Vowel: / yōō / u-e • Reading Words

Phonics Practice Book

Name _____

Write the word that names each picture.

goat	cube	kite	cake	leaf
train	deer	cone	night	

1

_____

2

_____

3

_____

4

_____

5

_____

6

_____

7

_____

8

_____

9

_____

Name _____

Read the story, and answer the questions.

ACROSS THE SEA

One fine day Joan, Pete, and Ray sailed out to sea. Their boat rolled over waves as they made their way east. They felt the sun's heat on their hair and a breeze on their cheeks. Then the waves started to grow.

"Oh no!" shouted Pete. "Our boat has a leak! Grab a pail and start to bail while I look for the hole." The hole was huge, but Pete plugged it up tight with boards from a crate. Then they sailed into a cove and rested. They watched whales and seals swim.

1. What happened to the boat when the waves got big?

_____

_____

2. What did Joan, Pete, and Ray do about the leak?

_____

_____

_____

Name _____

Fill in the circle next to the name of each picture.

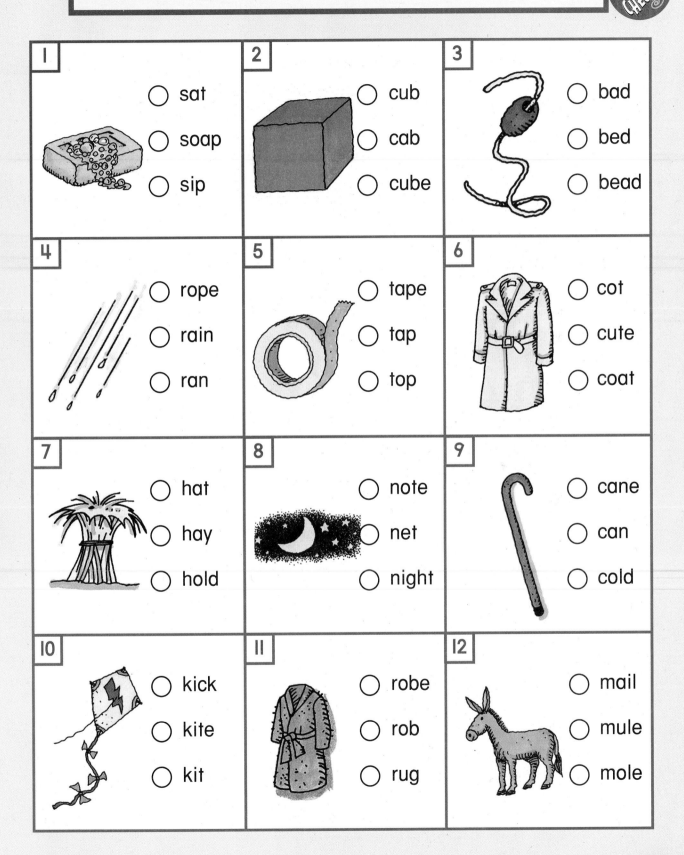

1
- ○ sat
- ○ soap
- ○ sip

2
- ○ cub
- ○ cab
- ○ cube

3
- ○ bad
- ○ bed
- ○ bead

4
- ○ rope
- ○ rain
- ○ ran

5
- ○ tape
- ○ tap
- ○ top

6
- ○ cot
- ○ cute
- ○ coat

7
- ○ hat
- ○ hay
- ○ hold

8
- ○ note
- ○ net
- ○ night

9
- ○ cane
- ○ can
- ○ cold

10
- ○ kick
- ○ kite
- ○ kit

11
- ○ robe
- ○ rob
- ○ rug

12
- ○ mail
- ○ mule
- ○ mole

Name _____

Fill in the circle next to the sentence that tells about each picture.

1
- ○ Dave meets a goat.
- ○ Jake eats his meal.
- ○ Mike takes the mail.

2
- ○ A snake meets a snail.
- ○ A seal dreams of the sea.
- ○ A snail makes a snack.

3
- ○ The blue jay sees a kite.
- ○ A jay plays with a rope.
- ○ He has a seed in his beak.

4
- ○ Fido eats ice cubes.
- ○ Fido's bone floats away.
- ○ Fido's nose is bright.

5
- ○ The mule uses a light at night.
- ○ The light shines in a hole.
- ○ The mule will find green grapes.

6
- ○ Rose paints a gate gray.
- ○ Joan uses soap on the sheep.
- ○ Kate makes a goat from clay.

Name _____

1	A can or a cane?	
2	A bed or a bead?	
3	A kit or a kite?	
4	A cot or a coat?	
5	Ran or rain?	
6	A pad or paid?	
7	A cub or a cube?	
8	A pin or a pine?	

Name _____

Read each word. Add a vowel to make it a word with a long vowel sound. Draw a picture for each new word.

1 set	_____ ------------------- _____	
2 can	_____ ------------------- _____	
3 cut	_____ ------------------- _____	
4 got	_____ ------------------- _____	
5 pin	_____ ------------------- _____	
6 ran	_____ ------------------- _____	

Harcourt Brace School Publishers

Name _____

fish	skates
cone	sun
bike	sled

What Is It?

1 You ride it. It has two wheels.

_____

2 You can't use it on a hot day!

_____

3 You can feed it at the pond.
It is not a duck.

_____

4 You go fast with these on your feet.

_____

5 Fill this with ice cream, and eat it!

_____

6 It shines bright and makes you hot.

_____

Name _____

Bow has the long **o** sound. Write **ow** for each picture whose name has the long **o** sound. Then trace the whole word.

bow

1. b o w

2. r

3. s n

4. h

5. m

6. b l

7. t r

8. b l

Long Vowel: / ō / ow

Phonics Practice Book

Name _____

Circle the word that completes each sentence. Then write the word.

1	_____ _____ us what Jean gave you!	Show She Shop
2	Do you think they _____ will _____?	glide glow glad
3	_____ What a big _____!	bow bee boat
4	_____ Can he _____ them all out?	blame blot blow
5	I can play in _____ the _____!	snap snail snow
6	How much did _____ you _____?	gray grow grin

Long Vowel: / ō / ow

Name _____

break The words **break** and **eight** have the long **a** sound. Write the word that names each picture.

8 eight

neigh	steak	weigh	eight
great	freight	sleigh	break	weight

1. weight

2. _____

3. _____

4. _____

5. _____

6. _____

7. _____

8. _____

9. _____

Long Vowel: / ā / ea, ei(gh)

Phonics Practice Book

Write the word that completes each sentence.

(neigh   break   great   sleigh   steak   eight)

_____
----

1. It is fun to ride in a _____.

_____
----

2. All _____ of us ride together.

_____
----

3. We are having a _____ time.

_____
----

4. The horses _____ as we ride along.

_____
----

5. Watch out! That window might _____!

_____
----

6. Mr. Green will take home a _____.

Name _____

Say the name of the first picture in the row. Color each picture whose name begins with the same sounds.

1 broom

2 truck

3 drop

4 frame

5 grin

6 crab

Name _____

Write the two letters that complete each picture name.
Then trace the other letters to write the whole word.

| br | cr | dr | fr | gr | pr | tr |

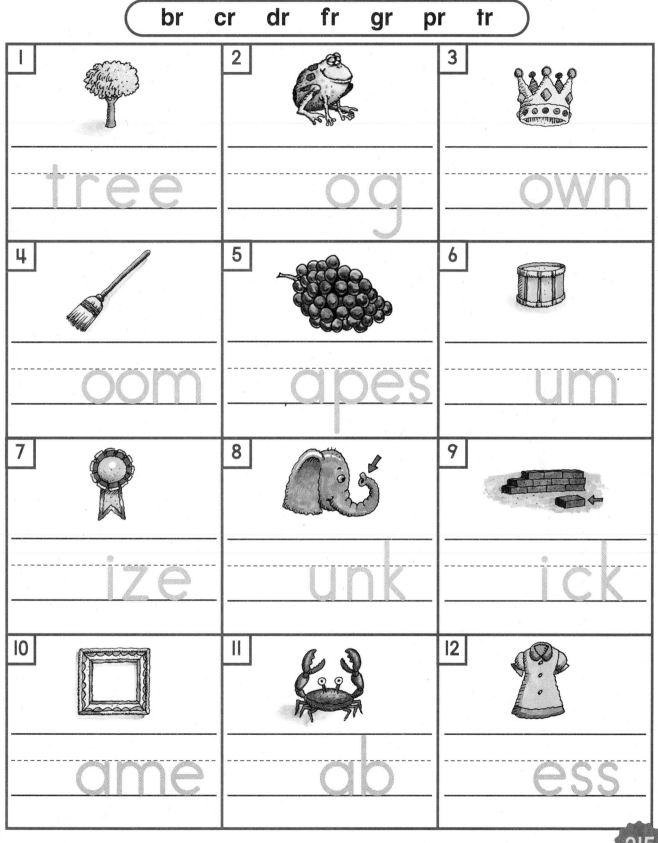

1. _____ tree

2. _____ og

3. _____ own

4. _____ oom

5. _____ apes

6. _____ um

7. _____ ize

8. _____ unk

9. _____ ick

10. _____ ame

11. _____ ab

12. _____ ess

Name _____

Circle the sentence that tells about each picture.

1	Fran sees a big frog. Fran sees a big crack. Fran sees a high track.
2	She sees a trap. She drops a top. She sees a crab.
3	Do not grab it! The crab will drop! Prop it up for me!
4	A trap is in the crack. A crab is in the trap. A crab will grab the dog.
5	Do not trot on the track. Do not grab the frog. Do not drop the trap.

Initial Clusters with *r* • Reading Words in Context

Look at each picture. Circle the word that completes the sentence. Then write the word.

1	Fran and her dog go to the _____ _____ .	track trip tap
2	The dog sees a big _____ _____ .	crack cap crab
3	He will not go in the _____ _____ .	top trap tap
4	Fran sees a _____ _____ .	dot dock drop
5	She will _____ _____ her dog.	green grab gap

Name _____

Say the name of the first picture in the row. Color the pictures whose names begin with the same sounds.

1 clam

2 plate

3 fly

4 blouse

5 play

6 clay

Initial Clusters with /

Phonics Practice Book

Harcourt Brace School Publishers

Name _____

Write the two letters that complete each picture name.
Then trace the whole word.

bl   cl   fl   pl

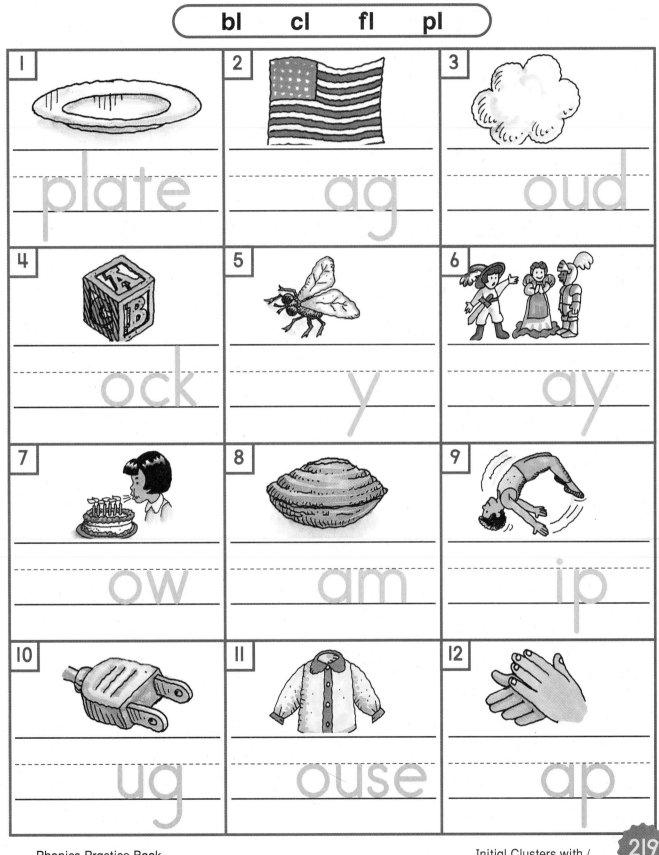

1 plate

2 ag

3 oud

4 ock

5 y

6 ay

7 ow

8 am

9 ip

10 ug

11 ouse

12 ap

Name _____

Look at each picture. Circle the word that completes the sentence. Then write the word.

1	_____ - - - - - - - - - - - - - - - - Look at the _____.	click clock crack
2	_____ - - - - - - - - - - - - - - - - The _____ came out!	plug pig play
3	_____ - - - - - - - - - - - - - - - - Did the _____ do this?	bus block blue
4	It's time to put up the _____ - - - - - - - - - - - - - - - - _____ .	flock flag fog
5	Everybody will _____ - - - - - - - - - - - - - - - - _____ now.	cap clip clap

Initial Clusters with *l* • Reading Words

Phonics Practice Book

Name _____

Circle the sentence that tells about each picture.

1	A flag is next to the plug.
	A clock is on the table.
	A plant grows in the window.

2	Fluff sees a fly.
	Fluff sees a clip.
	Fluff sees a blue top.

3	The flag is up.
	The clock will go down.
	The plum is blue.

4	The clip will flop.
	The fly will flip.
	The block will plop.

5	Fluff can clap!
	Fluff can flip!
	Fluff can plan!

Name _____

Write the two letters that complete each picture name.
Then trace the whole word.

br	cr	dr	fr	gr
pr	tr	bl	cl	fl	pl

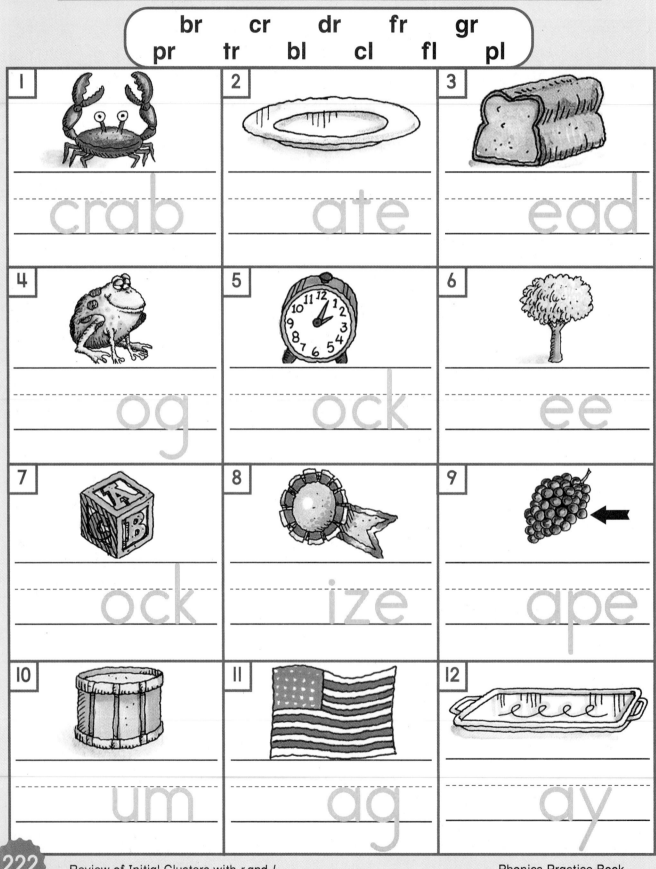

1 crab

2 ate

3 ead

4 og

5 ock

6 ee

7 ock

8 ize

9 ape

10 um

11 ag

12 ay

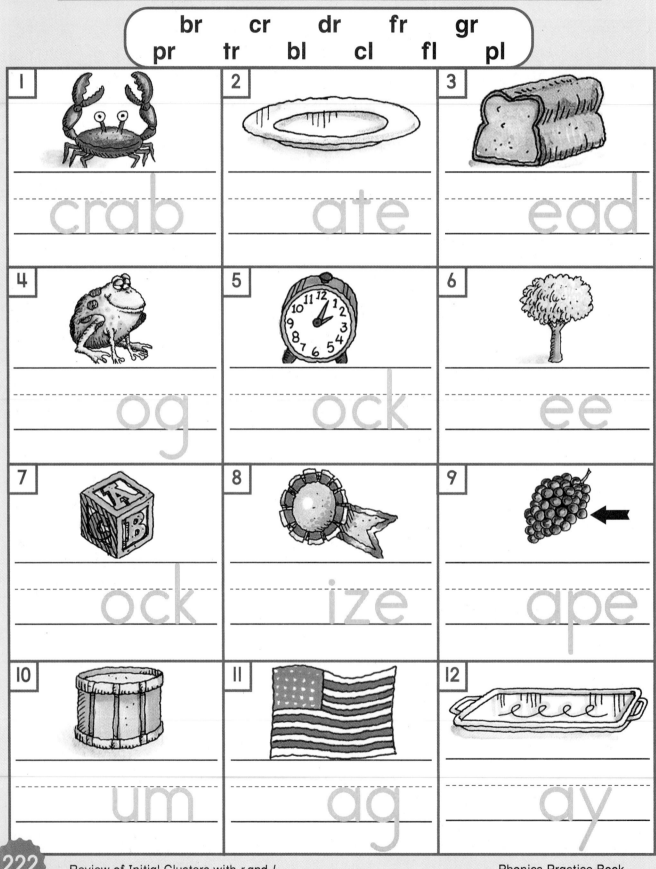

Review of Initial Clusters with *r* and *l*

Phonics Practice Book

Name _____

Write the word that completes each sentence.

| frog | clock | truck | grin | drum | blocks |

1.
_____

Fred will get a _____.

2.
_____

The baby likes the _____.

3.
_____

Here is a _____.

4.
_____

Fran plays with a _____.

5.
_____

The clown makes them _____.

6.
_____

Make the _____ hop.

Harcourt Brace School Publishers

Name _____

Say the name of the first picture in the row. Color the pictures whose names end with the same sounds.

1	ne**st**				
2	pr**int**				
3	sa**lt**				
4	li**ft**				
5	be**st**				

Harcourt Brace School Publishers

Name _____

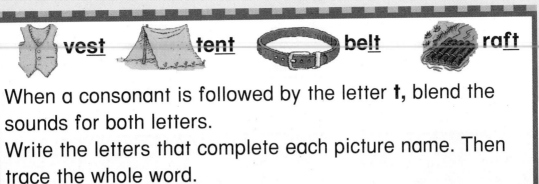
When a consonant is followed by the letter **t,** blend the sounds for both letters.

Write the letters that complete each picture name. Then trace the whole word.

st   nt   lt   ft

1. tent

2. gi

3. me

4. ne

5. toa

6. qui

7. li

8. pla

9. che

Harcourt Brace School Publishers

Circle the word that completes each sentence. Then write the word.

1	What can this _____ _____ be?	get gift goat
2	Can I have a _____ _____?	hit hint hen
3	It has a big _____ _____.	bell boat belt
4	And here is a _____ _____ , too.	vest vet vote
5	I like this dress the _____ _____.	bet bed best

Name _____

Read the poem. Then write a word from the poem to complete each sentence.

Walt Against Taft

Walt the colt could run so fast,

His friends saw a blur when he ran past.

"At running," said Walt, "I am the best."

Till Taft the duck put him to the test.

To the big oak and back they went.

Walt was swift and Taft looked spent.

Taft said to himself, "Go faster! You must!"

And he ran past Walt in a puff of dust.

_____

1. Walt said he was the _____ runner.

2. _____ is the duck who ran with Walt.

3. _____ won the race.

Name _____

Say the name of the first picture in the row. Color the pictures whose names end with the same sounds.

1. **sta<u>mp</u>**

2. **be<u>nd</u>**

3. **bui<u>ld</u>**

4. **bu<u>mp</u>**

5. **sa<u>nd</u>**

Final Clusters: *ld, mp, nd*

Phonics Practice Book

Name _____

 co<u>ld</u>   **la<u>mp</u>**   **ha<u>nd</u>**

When **ld**, **mp**, or **nd** are together at the end of a word, blend the sounds for both consonants. Write the letters that complete each picture name. Then trace the whole word.

| ld | mp | nd |

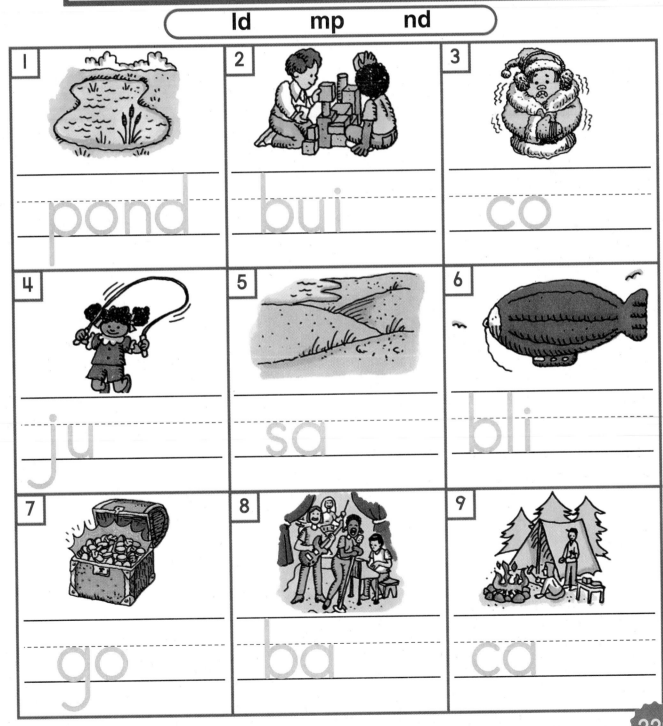

1. pond

2. bui

3. co

4. ju

5. sa

6. bli

7. go

8. ba

9. ca

Circle the sentence that tells about the picture.

1	I found gold on the ground. I told you there was a blimp. I will hold the plant for you.
2	He will not jump in the pond. One boy found a dump truck. They like to play with sand.
3	Can a child jump over this? Can we mend this lamp? Can you find one with a good band?
4	What is in this old trunk? Is there a lump of sand? Who held that lamp for you?
5	Let's hold on to the stump. Let's rake the damp leaves. Let's find the wild ducks.
6	I hit the ground with my hand. This old tree does not bend. We found this old tent.

Final Clusters: *ld, mp, nd* • Reading Words in Context

Phonics Practice Book

Read the poem. Then write a word from the poem to complete each sentence.

CIRCUS DAY

They like to stamp their feet—thump, thump!

The clowns run up the ramp and jump.

I love to hear the circus band.

The music makes me clap my hands.

Sitting here with my best friend,

I wish it did not have to end.

1. The clowns run up a _____ .

2. Then they _____ off.

3. We wish the circus would never _____ .

REVIEW

Write the letters that complete each picture name. Then trace the whole word.

| st | nt | lt | ft | ld | mp | nd |

1. nest

2. la

3. te

4. co

5. gi

6. ha

7. be

8. ju

9. pla

10. ve

11. po

12. qui

Review of Final Clusters

Phonics Practice Book

Name _____

Circle the sentence that tells about each picture.

1
I will lend you my gold belt.
Let's hunt and see what we find.
They felt cold at the pond.

2
Walk past these wild animals.
Come and jump on this raft.
Look at the dust on this chest.

3
Will you help me fold this quilt?
Who told you about this nest?
Will you send me a little gift?

4
He has a cast on his hand.
We can mend that nest.
That vest is just too big.

5
The lamp is in an old tent.
There is rust on this old lamp.
The pump is too bent to mend.

6
We must work together to lift it.
We can camp out in this tent.
We will rest here on the sand.

Say the name of the first picture in each row. Color the pictures whose names begin with the same sounds.

1. snail

2. smell

3. stamp

4. ski

5. sleep

6. spin

Initial Clusters with *s*

Phonics Practice Book

Name _____

When **s** is followed by a consonant (that is not **h**), blend the sounds for both letters.

Circle each picture name. Then write the word.

snack **sm**ile **sc**arf **sk**i **sl**ide **sp**oon

1. sped
(sled)
said

sled

2. skate
ski
sky

3. soap
scamp
stamp

4. scoop
stop
slope

5. skin
spin
pin

6. smoke
soak
spoke

7. sap
slap
snap

8. steep
sleep
seep

9. sick
slick
stick

Initial Clusters with *s*

Name _____

Circle the sentence that tells about each picture.

1

Jack and Jill stand on the hill.
Jack and Jill skip up the hill.
Jack and Jill sleep on the hill.

2

This hill is too steep!
This stone is so big!
This sled will not stop!

3

They spend time on a stump.
They smell smoke from the stove.
They stop for water and a snack.

4

They ask the snail to stop smiling.
They don't let the snake scare them.
They spend the day on skis and sleds.

5

Jack sniffs and gets a stick.
Jack speaks and stands still.
Jack slips and the water spills.

6

Jill's skill keeps the water in.
Jill sits still and smiles.
Jill needs a scarf for the snow.

Harcourt Brace School Publishers

Initial Clusters with *s* • Reading Words in Context

Phonics Practice Book

Name _____

FRIENDS

We are friends. We skip together. We slide on a sled in the snow. When we dance, we turn and spin. We stay snug in our scarfs. But best of all, we smile when we're together!

_____

1. You slide on a ————— in the snow.

_____

2. You can be ————— in a scarf.

_____

3. You have a big ————— when you're happy.

Now write about what you and a friend like to do.

_____

_____

_____

Name _____

Say the name of the first picture in the row. Color each picture whose name begins with the same sounds.

1 swim

2 twins

3 sweater

4 twist

Initial Clusters with *w*

Phonics Practice Book

swing

twig

When **s** or **t** is followed by a **w**, blend the sounds of both letters. Write **sw** or **tw** to complete each picture name. Then trace the whole word.

1. _____ swing

2. _____ an

3. _____ ig

4. _____ eep

5. _____ elve

6. _____ im

7. _____ ins

8. _____ eater

9. _____ ist

10. _____ enty

11. _____ ine

12. _____ itch

Name _____

Write the letters that complete each picture name. Then trace the whole word.

1	2	3
nest	ick	og

4	5	6
qui	ar	ain

7	8	9
la	ize	ist

10	11	12
ing	be	ed

Harcourt Brace School Publishers

Name _____

Do what the sentences tell you.

1. Find the frog that is on land. Draw spots on it.

2. Draw a raft in the pond.

3. Color the sky bright blue.

4. Draw a green plant in the grass.

5. Find a nest on a tree branch. Draw a twig for the nest.

6. Mr. Grant stands and paints. Draw a tree in Mr. Grant's frame.

7. Fran smiles and claps her hands. Circle Fran.

CHECK-UP

Fill in the circle next to the word that names each picture.

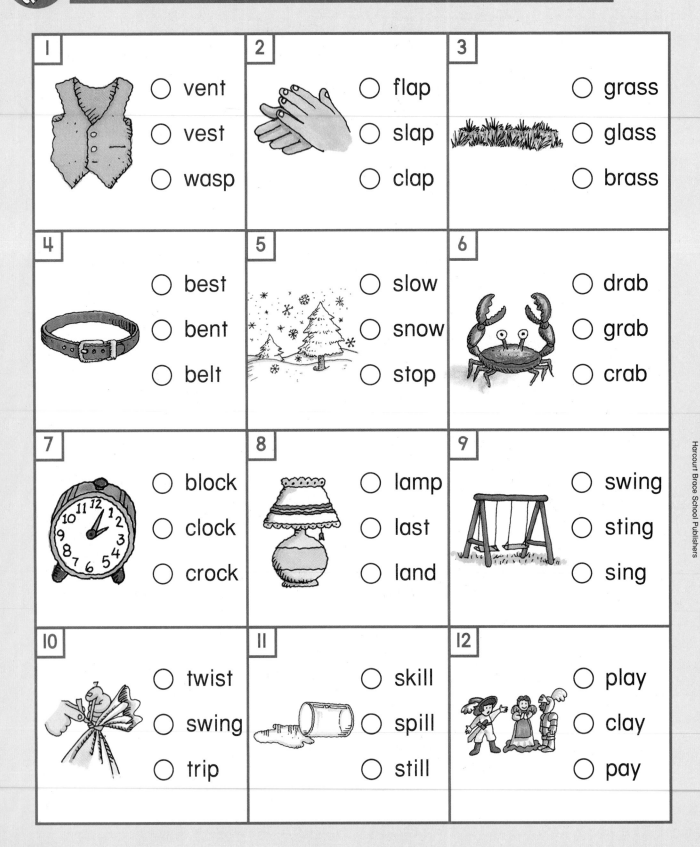

1.
- ○ vent
- ○ vest
- ○ wasp

2.
- ○ flap
- ○ slap
- ○ clap

3.
- ○ grass
- ○ glass
- ○ brass

4.
- ○ best
- ○ bent
- ○ belt

5.
- ○ slow
- ○ snow
- ○ stop

6.
- ○ drab
- ○ grab
- ○ crab

7.
- ○ block
- ○ clock
- ○ crock

8.
- ○ lamp
- ○ last
- ○ land

9.
- ○ swing
- ○ sting
- ○ sing

10.
- ○ twist
- ○ swing
- ○ trip

11.
- ○ skill
- ○ spill
- ○ still

12.
- ○ play
- ○ clay
- ○ pay

Harcourt Brace School Publishers

Consonant Clusters Test

Phonics Practice Book

Name _____

Fill in the circle next to the sentence that tells about the picture.

1

○ We must play on the swings.
○ One day we went to the pond.
○ Plants are not growing in the snow.

2

○ A plum fell and stuck on a stick.
○ A fly felt cold and went in the tent.
○ A frog jumps and lands with a plop.

3

○ It spins fast and slides down.
○ A snake slips under a stone.
○ A snail went into its nest.

4

○ It holds a stick in its hand.
○ The fly stays on the stump.
○ A fly lands on a twig.

5

○ They hunt for gold in the pond.
○ Wild animals stop here to drink.
○ My mother told them to sleep.

6

○ Look at the clam and the crab.
○ A fish does a flip and swims away.
○ It can go fast and fly to a tree.

Harcourt Brace School Publishers

Color each picture whose name begins with the same sounds as **quack**.

q<u>u</u>ack

Initial Digraph: / kw / *qu*

Phonics Practice Book

Name _____

quack

Say the name of each picture. If it begins with the same sounds as **quack,** write **qu.** Then trace the whole word.

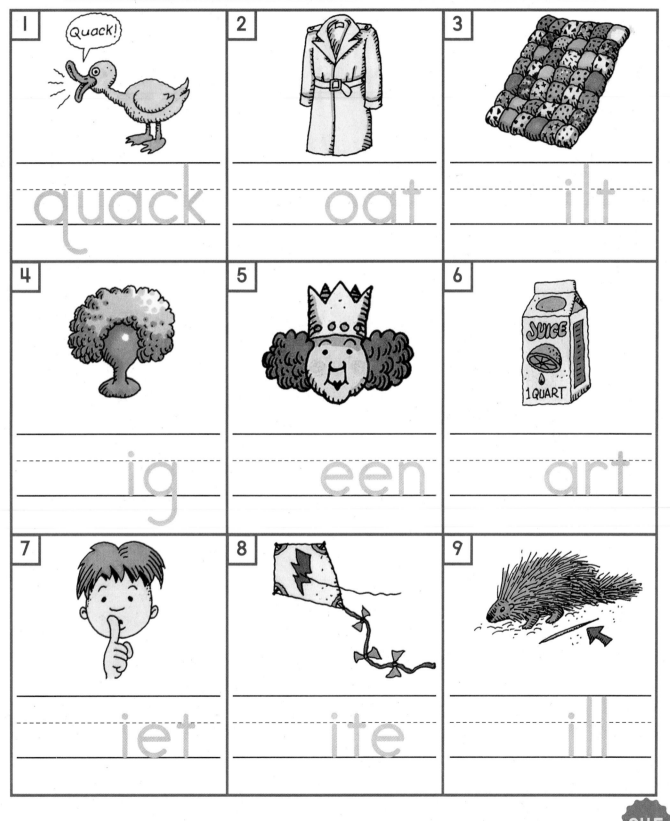

1	2	3
Quack! quack	oat	ilt
4	5	6
ig	een	art
7	8	9
iet	ite	ill

Name _____

Color each picture whose name begins with the same sound as **chair**.

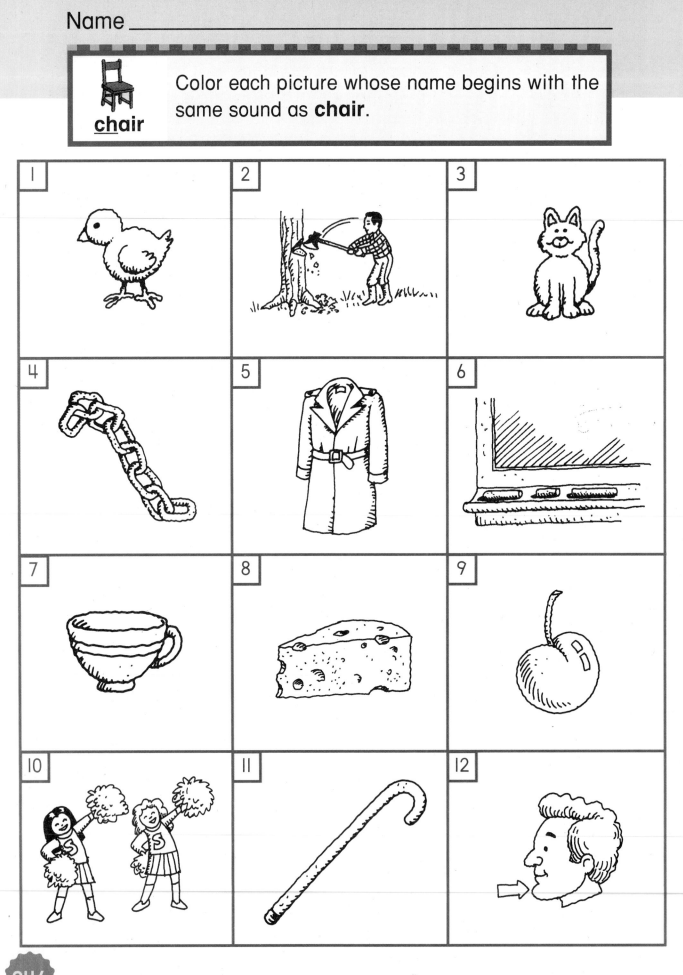

Initial Digraph: / ch / ch

Phonics Practice Book

chair

Say the name of each picture. If it begins with the same sound as **chair,** write **ch.** Then trace the whole word.

1. chair

2. ap

3. eck

4. one

5. op

6. ake

7. ick

8. eer

9. alk

Initial Digraph: / ch / *ch*

Name _____

1	2	3
4	5	6
7	8	9

Name _____

match

Say the name of each picture. If it ends with the same sound as **match**, write **tch.** Then trace the whole word.

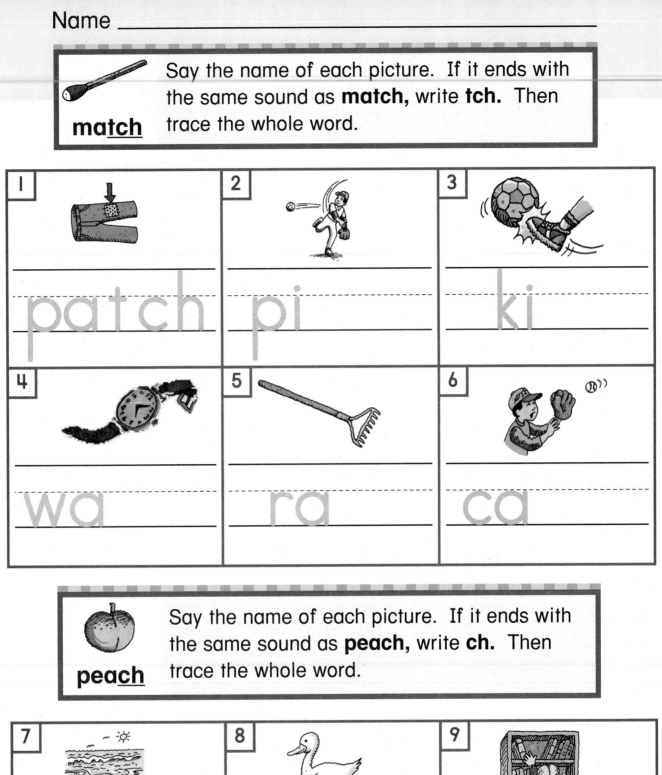

1. pa**tch**	2. pi___	3. ki___
4. wa___	5. ra___	6. ca___

peach

Say the name of each picture. If it ends with the same sound as **peach**, write **ch.** Then trace the whole word.

7. bea___	8. du___	9. rea___

Harcourt Brace School Publishers

Phonics Practice Book

Final Digraph: / ch / ch, tch

249

Name _____

think

Color each picture whose name begins with the same sound as **think**.

1	2	3
4	5	6
7	8	9

Harcourt Brace School Publishers

Initial Digraph: / th / *th*

Phonics Practice Book

Name _____

think

Say the name of each picture. If it begins with the same sound as **think,** write **th.** Then trace the whole word.

1	2	3
___ think	___ umb	___ ack
4	5	6
___ oast	___ orn	___ ird
7	8	9
___ irty	___ op	___ imble

Name _____

too<u>th</u>

Color each picture whose name ends with the same sound as **tooth**.

1.

2.

3.

4.

5.

6.

7.

8.

9.

Name _____

tooth

Say the name of each picture. If it ends with the same sound as **tooth**, write **th**. Then trace the whole word.

1	2	3
ba	coa	too

4	5	6
pa	wrea	ba

7	8	9
clo	fee	boo

Name _____

Circle and write the letters that complete each picture name. Then trace the whole word.

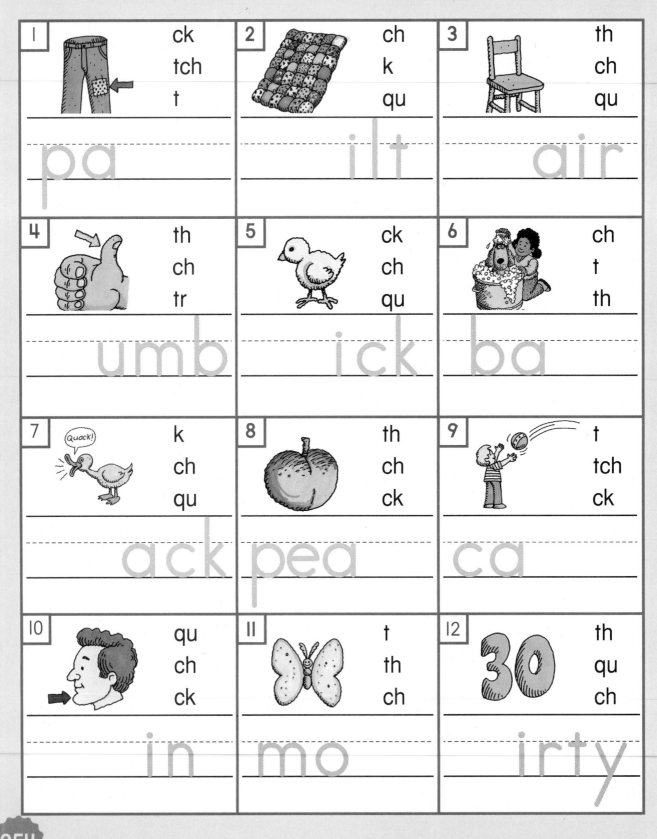

1	ck tch t	pa___
2	ch k qu	___ilt
3	th ch qu	___air
4	th ch tr	___umb
5	ck ch qu	ch___ick
6	ch t th	ba___
7	k ch qu	___ack
8	th ch ck	pea___
9	t tch ck	ca___
10	qu ch ck	___in
11	t th ch	mo___
12	th qu ch	___irty

Review of Digraphs / kw / *qu;* / ch / *ch, tch;* / th / *th*

Phonics Practice Book

Harcourt Brace School Publishers

Name _____

Mitch and the Ducks

There once was a pony named Mitch

Who chased thirty ducks to the ditch.

Each duck gave a quack,

And thumped Mitch on the back,

Till he didn't know which duck was which.

1. Where did Mitch chase the ducks?

_____

- -

_____

_____

- -

_____

2. What did the ducks do?

_____

- -

_____

_____

- -

_____

Name _____

ship

Color each picture whose name begins with the same sound as **ship**.

Initial Digraph: / sh / *sh*

Phonics Practice Book

ship

Say the name of each picture. If it begins with the same sound as **ship**, write **sh.** Then trace the whole word.

1	2	3
ship	un	ell
4 irt	**5** oe	**6** ock
7 ick	**8** eep	**9** ave
10 elf	**11** eal	**12** ade

Initial Digraph: / sh / *sh*

257

bush

Color each picture whose name ends with the same sound as **bush.**

Final Digraph: / sh / *sh*

Phonics Practice Book

bush

Say the name of each picture. If it ends with the same sound as **bush,** write **sh.** Then trace the whole word.

1 di**sh**	2 pu___	3 ki___
4 lea___	5 ga___	6 fi___
7 gla___	8 bru___	9 spla___
10 wa___	11 bu___	12 tra___

Name _____

whale

Circle and color each picture whose name begins with the same sound as **whale.**

Initial Digraph: / hw /*wh*

Phonics Practice Book

Harcourt Brace School Publishers

whale

Say the name of each picture. If it begins with the sound for **wh,** write **wh.** Then trace the whole word.

1	2
___ ale	___ isper

3	4
___ ick	___ ite

5	6
___ ell	___ een

7	8
___ istle	___ iskers

Initial Digraph: / hw / *wh* **261**

Name _____

REVIEW

Circle and write the letters that complete each picture name. Then trace the whole word.

1. ch sh wh — _____ eep

2. wh sh qu — _____ ale

3. wh th sh — _____ ed

4. th wh ch — _____ eel

5. ch th sh — _____ oe

6. ch sh qu — _____ ip

7. sh wh th — _____ di

8. wh ch qu — _____ ite

9. ch wh sh — _____ elf

10. th wh qu — _____ istle

11. sh wh th — _____ ave

12. wh th sh — _____ irt

Harcourt Brace School Publishers

Name _____

1	When will the sheep find a dish? Why is the sheep on a ship? Which ship will be in a shop?
2	The fish found some trash. The whale wanted a brush. The whale found a shell.
3	Move the wheel to move the ship. Shut the window on the ship. Brush the sheep and stop the ship.
4	See it push and whisper. Watch it flash and shine. Watch the waves crash to shore.
5	Why did you crush my dish? Where can I shop for a brush? What do you wish to eat?
6	Here is a dish of fresh greens. The fish sits on a white shed. Ask the whale to crush the shells.

SUPER REVIEW

Circle and write the letters that complete each picture name. Then trace the whole word.

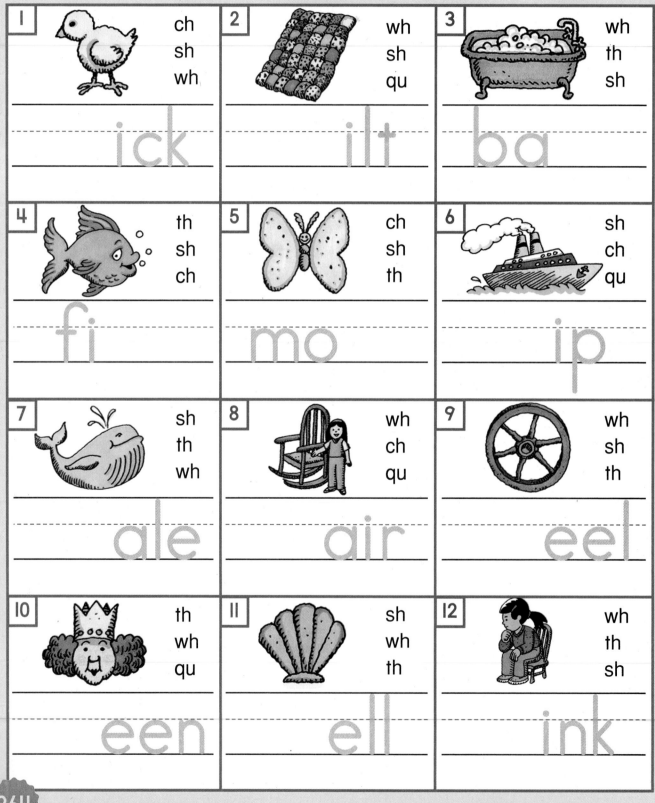

1. ch sh wh — ick

2. wh sh qu — ilt

3. wh th sh — ba

4. th sh ch — fi

5. ch sh th — mo

6. sh ch qu — ip

7. sh th wh — ale

8. wh ch qu — air

9. wh sh th — eel

10. th wh qu — een

11. sh wh th — ell

12. wh th sh — ink

Harcourt Brace School Publishers

Cumulative Review of Digraphs

Phonics Practice Book

Name _____

Do what the sentences tell you.

1. Which chick is in a bath? Draw a brush for him.

2. Find the chick with the itch on her chin. Circle her.

3. Chip chats with Dan. Dan quacks. Color Chip.

4. A chick will hatch soon! Color the shell.

5. Which one will Chuck catch? It is white now. Color it blue.

6. Chad went to the shed. Draw a path to help him come back.

CHECK-UP

Fill in the circle next to the name of each picture.

1
- ○ shore
- ○ chop
- ○ crop

2
- ○ catch
- ○ cloth
- ○ cast

3
- ○ patch
- ○ path
- ○ past

4
- ○ sip
- ○ ship
- ○ whip

5
- ○ bath
- ○ beach
- ○ bush

6
- ○ chick
- ○ thick
- ○ quick

7
- ○ bath
- ○ batch
- ○ band

8
- ○ thin
- ○ chin
- ○ shin

9
- ○ whistle
- ○ thirty
- ○ branch

10
- ○ wash
- ○ went
- ○ west

11
- ○ shoe
- ○ still
- ○ quilt

12
- ○ thorn
- ○ shelf
- ○ chick

Harcourt Brace School Publishers

Name _____

Fill in the circle next to the sentence that goes with each picture.

1

○ Both sandwiches are too thin.

○ Why is your sandwich so thick?

○ What did you pitch in the trash?

2

○ We have to rush to the ship.

○ We have to check the fish.

○ We have to dash to catch the bus.

3

○ They brush the dog's chin.

○ It's time for a quick bath.

○ The dog likes to have a dish.

4

○ This dish is for the chicks.

○ The chicks are on a branch.

○ They have a dish for the sheep.

5

○ Let's get them out of the shed.

○ Let's quit watching the shop.

○ Let's chase them into the garden.

Harcourt Brace School Publishers

Name _____

Say the names of the pictures in each row. Color the pictures whose names rhyme.

R-controlled Vowel: / är / • Phonemic Awareness

Phonics Practice Book

Harcourt Brace School Publishers

Color the pictures that have the sound you hear at the end of  and in the middle of .

Name_____

car

Write **ar** to complete each picture name that has the sound you hear at the end of **car.** Then trace the whole word.

1 tar	2 c___p	3 c___t
4 j___	5 b___n	6 h___t
7 n___l	8 ___m	9 st___
10 c___n	11 c___d	12 p___k

R-controlled Vowel: / är / ar

Harcourt Brace School Publishers

Phonics Practice Book

Name _____

Write the name of each picture.

1. bar

2.

3.

4.

5.

6.

7.

8.

9.

10.

11.

12.

Name _____

tar

Write the picture names that rhyme with tar.
Then add one more rhyming word and a picture.

1.

b<u>ar</u>

2.

3.

4.

R-controlled Vowel: / är / *ar* • Phonograms

Phonics Practice Book

Name _____

1. b a r n

2. p a r k

3. s t a r

4. c a r t

5. c a r

Name _____

Write **ar** to complete each word. Then trace the whole word and draw a picture for the word.

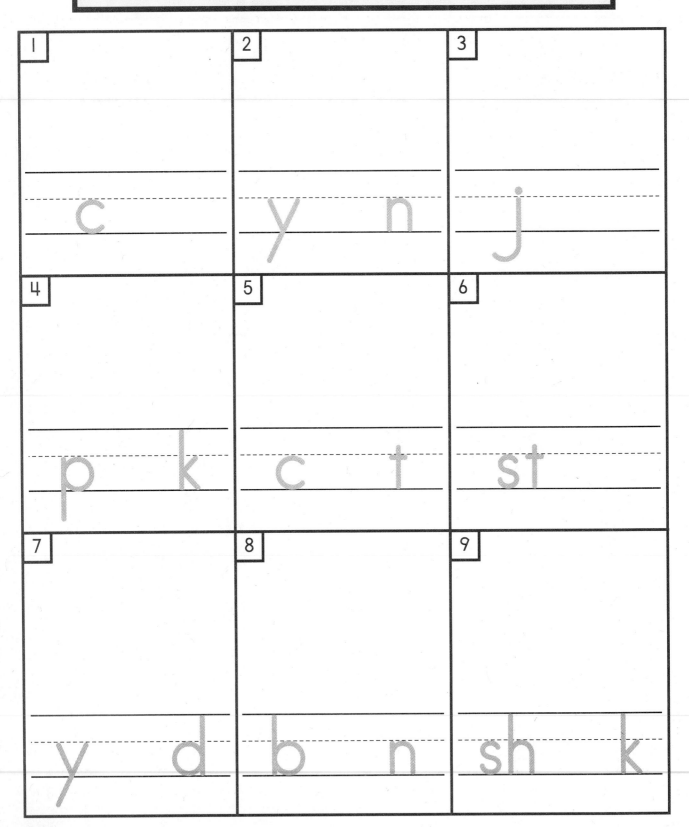

1	2	3
c ___ ___	y ___ ___ n	j ___ ___
4	5	6
p ___ ___ k	c ___ ___ t	___ ___ st
7	8	9
y ___ ___ d	b ___ ___ n	sh ___ ___ k

Harcourt Brace School Publishers

R-controlled Vowel: /är/ / ar • Reading Words

Phonics Practice Book

Name _____

| park | car | barn | card | far | farm |

1

My friend Mark moved

_____

_____

_____ away.

2

We played together in the

_____

_____ .

3

Now he lives on a

_____

_____ .

4

There are cows in his

_____

_____ .

5

Soon we will go there in our

_____

_____ .

6

Right now, I can make a

_____

_____ for Mark.

Name _____

Marty's Party

Barb and Mark were going to a party.

It was a surprise for their friend Marty.

That cold March morning, they walked in the yard,

Pulling their scarves on, the wind blowing hard,

Thinking, "Why does Marty have to live far?"

"How come we couldn't ride there in a car?"

When they got to Marty's, the party could start.

They all had a great time. That Marty was smart.

They played with his puppy till it started to bark.

They played and they danced until it was dark.

What did the friends do at Marty's party?

_____

_____

_____

_____

Name _____

1. Spark barks a lot. Color Spark.
2. Find the pony, Star. Draw a cart for Star.
3. Mr. Clark parks his car next to the barn.
   Color the car.
4. Find someone with a scarf. Color the scarf green.
5. Karl works hard on the farm. Color Karl's
   jeans blue.

Name _____

Fill in the circle next to the sentence that tells about each picture.

1	○ Let's march to the park.
	○ Let's start by getting a cart.
	○ Let's get the tar off your arm.

2	○ It is hard to get this jar.
	○ I can't get to the barn.
	○ The jar is out in the yard.

3	○ These are made of yarn.
	○ Here are some cards.
	○ These grew on a farm.

4	○ There is a mark on my arm.
	○ These stars are dark.
	○ I like the one with stars.

5	○ Did the dog bark in the yard?
	○ Did we park the car far away?
	○ Did the cart do much harm?

Harcourt Brace School Publishers

R-Controlled Vowel: / är / ar Test   Phonics Practice Book

Name _____

A **contraction** is a word made by writing two words together and leaving out one or more letters. An **apostrophe** (') shows where letters were left out.

Color the block if the contraction stands for the two words below it.

I will = I'll

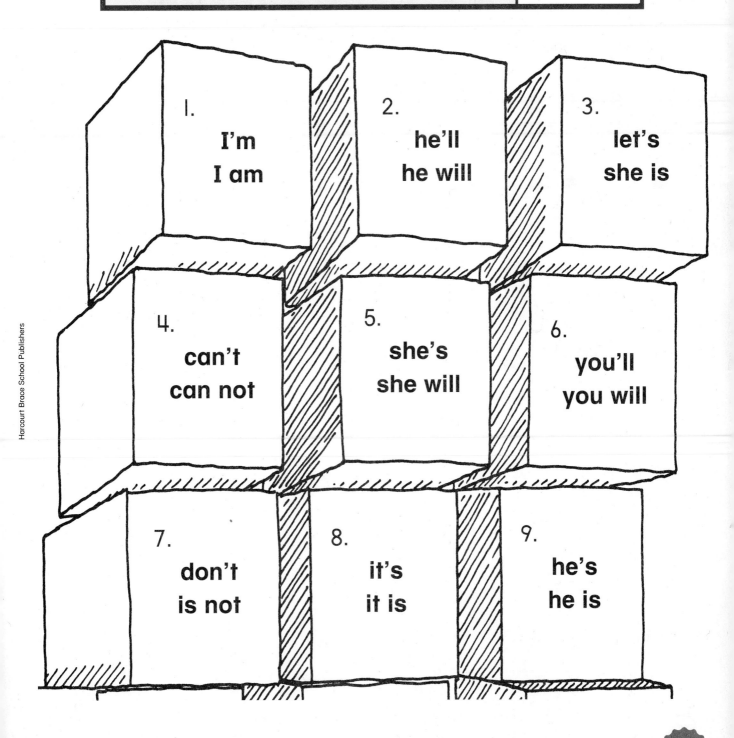

1. **I'm**
   I am

2. **he'll**
   he will

3. **let's**
   she is

4. **can't**
   can not

5. **she's**
   she will

6. **you'll**
   you will

7. **don't**
   is not

8. **it's**
   it is

9. **he's**
   he is

Name _____

Look at each picture and read the sentence. Write the contraction that stands for the underlined words.

she is = she's

I will = I'll

do not = don't

let us = let's

1 I will mix the cake.

_____

_____ mix the cake.

2 Do not come in here.

_____

_____ come in here.

3 I think she is going to like it.

_____

I think _____ going to like it.

4 Now let us eat it!

_____

Now _____ eat it.

Contractions: 'm, 'll, n't, 's

Phonics Practice Book

Name _____

We use **'s** to show that a thing belongs to someone.
Julie's hat is a **hat that belongs to Julie**.
Write the word that completes each sentence.

(sheep's   mother's   cow's   dog's   baby's)

_____
- -

1. The duck rides on the _____ back.

_____
- -

2. The dog rides on the _____ back.

_____
- -

3. There are spots on the _____ back.

_____
- -

4. The animals are in the _____ room.

_____
- -

5. There is a boat in the _____ hand.

Harcourt Brace School Publishers

Name _____

A **contraction** is a word made by writing two words together and leaving out a letter or letters. An **apostrophe** (') shows where letters were left out.
Color the hat if the contraction stands for the two words below it.

**I would =
I'd**

1	2	3
you've you have	we're we would	they'd they had

4	5	6
I'd I would	they've they have	you'd we would

7	8	9
she'd they are	we're we are	we'd we would

Contractions: 'd, 've, 're

Phonics Practice Book

Name _____

Look at each picture, and read the sentence. Write the contraction that stands for the underlined words.

I would = I'd   they would = they'd
we have = we've   you are = you're

1	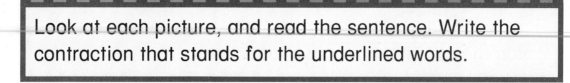	You are not going to sit down, are you? _____ - _____ not going to sit down, are you?
2		Yes, we have danced all night. _____ - - - - - - - - - - - - - - - - - - - Yes,_____ danced all night.
3		But I would like to dance more. _____ - - - - - - - - - - But _____ like to dance more.
4		I wish they would dance with me! _____ - I wish _____ dance with me!

Phonics Practice Book

Contractions: 'd, 've, 're

Name _____

Read each sentence. Fill in the circle next to the two words the contraction stands for.

1. This tree <u>isn't</u> very big.	○ is not ○ can not
2. <u>We're</u> going to plant it here.	○ We have ○ We are
3. <u>You've</u> found a good place.	○ You have ○ They have
4. <u>I'm</u> glad you like it.	○ I am ○ I will
5. <u>She'll</u> get some water for it.	○ She is ○ She will
6. <u>I'd</u> like to help, too.	○ I would ○ He would
7. <u>It's</u> fun to plant a little tree!	○ I have ○ It is

Name _____

Fill in the circle next to the sentence that tells about each picture.

1
- ○ The king found the duck's fork.
- ○ The animals sit at the king's table.
- ○ They are at the dog's window.

2
- ○ There is cake on the cow's fork.
- ○ There is cake on the dog's fork.
- ○ There is cake on the sheep's fork.

3
- ○ The king's scarf is on his head.
- ○ The horse's scarf is on the table.
- ○ The dog's scarf gets in the way.

4
- ○ The cow's feet are small.
- ○ The duck's feet are small.
- ○ The dog's feet are small.

5
- ○ The king takes the cow's water.
- ○ The king takes the duck's cake.
- ○ The king takes the horse's gift.

6
- ○ It was the cow's home.
- ○ It was the king's birthday.
- ○ It was the horse's birthday.

Name _____

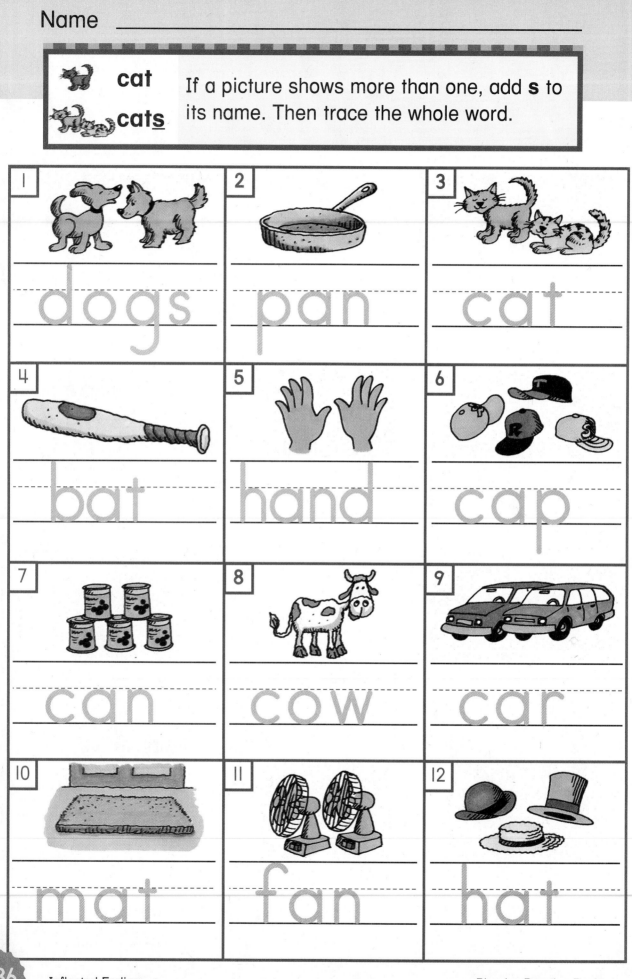

cat

cats

If a picture shows more than one, add **s** to its name. Then trace the whole word.

1. dogs

2. pan

3. cat

4. bat

5. hand

6. cap

7. can

8. cow

9. car

10. mat

11. fan

12. hat

Inflected Ending: -s

Phonics Practice Book

Harcourt Brace School Publishers

Name _____

Add **s** to most telling words that tell about one person, place, animal, or thing.

Add **s** to each word to make it tell about now. Then trace the whole word.

The cat jump<u>s</u>.

1

A girl ___ come ___ .

2

He ___ see ___ it.

3

The baby ___ clap ___ .

4

He ___ find ___ it.

Use a telling word with **s** in a sentence.

_____

_____

_____

Inflected Ending: -s

 287

Name_____

Now

We **walk** to school.

Past

We **walked** to school.

Add **ed** to each word to make it tell about the past. Then trace the whole word.

1. walked

2. play

3. snow

4. paint

Now write two sentences about something that happened in the past. Use words with **ed.**

_____

_____

_____

_____

Inflected Ending: -ed

Phonics Practice Book

Name _____

Find three words in the puzzle that end in **ed** and tell about the past. Circle the words. Then write the word from the puzzle that completes each sentence.

c	l	i	m	b	e	d
l	b	a	c	k	g	a
i	j	u	m	p	e	d
m	e	b	j	u	m	p
b	a	c	k	e	d	m

1

The cat _____ up.

_____
- - - - - - - - - - - - - - - - - - - -

2

The dog _____ out.

_____
- - - - - - - - - - - - - - - - - - - -

3

I _____ it in.

_____
- - - - - - - - - - - - - - - - - - - -

Inflected Ending: *-ed*

Name _____

I fly.  **I am flying.**

Add **ing** to each word to make a new word. Then trace the whole word.

1. climbing	2. rain
3. eat	4. cook

Now write two sentences that use **ing** words.

_____

- -

_____

- -

_____

Inflected Ending: *-ing*

Phonics Practice Book

Name _____

Circle and write the word that completes each sentence.

1	Do you see me _____ _____ up?	climbed climbing climbs
2	I am _____ _____ down.	jumping jumps jumped
3	I am _____ _____ out.	backs backed backing
4	My dog was _____ _____ my cap.	find finding finds
5	Did you like _____ _____ my dog?	seeing see sees

Name _____

Double the final letter of most words with short vowels before adding **ed.**
Double the final consonant and add **ed** to each word.
Then trace the whole word.

pop + p + ed = popped

1. hopped

2. pat

3. mop

4. grab

5. zip

6. drop

Harcourt Brace School Publishers

Name_____

Circle the word that completes the sentence. Then write the word.

1	Dan _____ Tip.	pat patted played
2	Tip _____ up on Dan.	hopped hop here
3	Then Dan _____ .	trip top tripped
4	Dan _____ Tip.	green grabbed grab
5	Dan and Tip both _____ .	dripped drips down

Double the final consonant of most words with short vowels before adding **ing.**

Double the final consonant and add **ing** to each word.

 pop + p + ing = popping

1. sitting

2. hop

3. drip

4. pat

5. drop

6. grin

Inflected Ending: -ing (double final consonant)

Phonics Practice Book

Harcourt Brace School Publishers

Name _____

Stepping Out

Heads nodding, feet tapping
Hands snapping and clapping
Playing and grinning,
We jump away spinning.
Hopping and bopping
Until we are dropping
No one is stopping.
Let's jump until two.

What is the poem about? How can you tell?

_____

- -

_____

- -

_____

Name _____

When a word ends with **e**, drop the final **e** before adding **ed**. Write words that tell about the past.

Drop the final **e** and add **ed** to each word.

chase − e + ed = chased

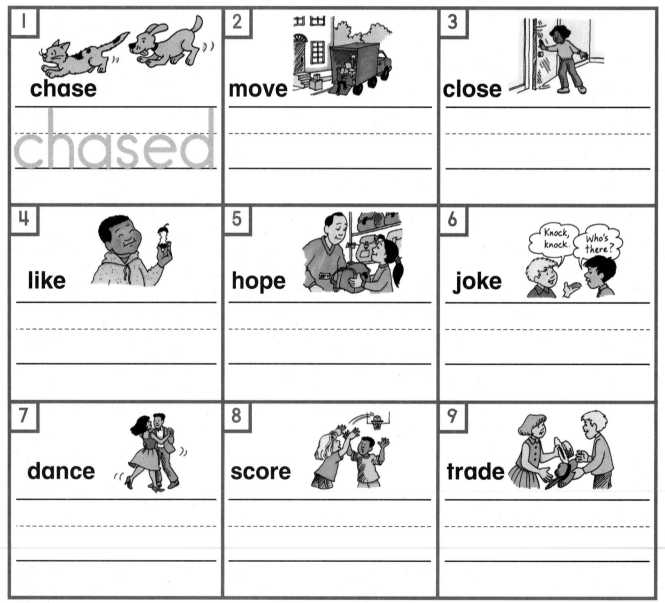

1. chase — chased

2. move _____

3. close _____

4. like _____

5. hope _____

6. joke _____

7. dance _____

8. score _____

9. trade _____

Inflected Ending: -ed (drop final e)

Phonics Practice Book

Harcourt Brace School Publishers

Name _____

Add **ed** to the words below to make them tell about the past.

move _____

----

hope _____

_____

surprise

_____

_____

dance

_____

Now use the words you wrote to complete the story.

The Day of the Ducks

_____

----

1. One day some ducks _____ into a house.

_____

----

2. That _____ me!

_____

----

3. Three little ducks _____ together.

_____

----

4. I _____ we could all be friends.

Inflected Ending: *-ed* (drop final *e*) **297**

When a word ends with **e**, drop the **e** before adding **ing**.
Write new words that tell about now.

Drop the final **e** and add **ing** to each word.

chase − e + ing = chasing

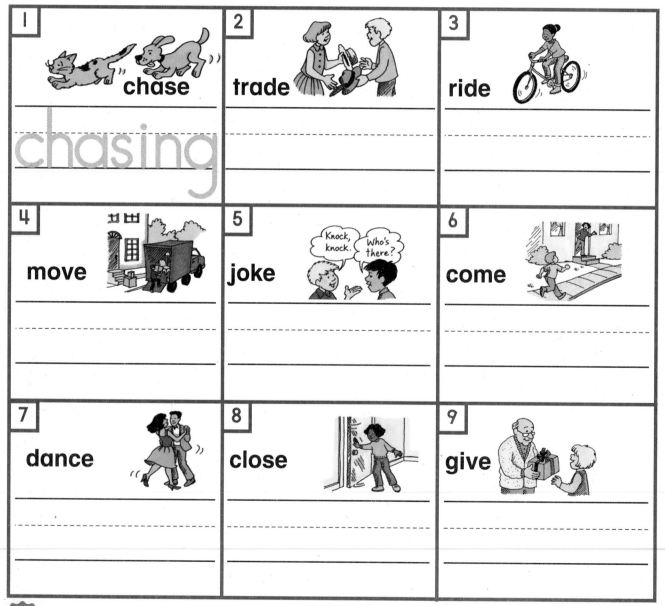

1 **chase**

chasing

2 **trade**

3 **ride**

4 **move**

5 **joke**

Knock, knock. Who's there?

6 **come**

7 **dance**

8 **close**

9 **give**

Inflected Ending: -*ing* (drop final *e*)

Phonics Practice Book

Name _____

Add **ing** to the words below. Then use the words you
wrote to complete the sentences.

dance

_____

- -

_____

ride

_____

- -

_____

come

_____

- -

_____

chase

_____

- -

_____

_____

- -

1. Look! My story friends are _____ out.

_____

- -

2. One is _____ a pony.

_____

- -

3. One is _____ her sheep.

_____

- -

4. One is _____ with a mouse.

Name _____

In a word that ends with **x, ch, sh,** or **s,** add **es** to tell about more than one or to tell about now.

Write **es** to make each picture name tell about more than one. Then trace the whole word.

two watch<u>es</u>   She watch<u>es</u> them play.
watch + es = watches

1 peach

2 dish

3 box

4 branch

Write the word that completes each sentence.

brushes   catches

5 1. He _____ the ball.

6 2. She _____ her dog.

Inflected Ending: -es   Phonics Practice Book

Name _____

teach	**hatch**
_____	_____
- - - - - - - - - - - - - - -	- - - - - - - - - - - - - - -
_____	_____
watch	**branch**
_____	_____
- - - - - - - - - - - - - - -	- - - - - - - - - - - - - - -
_____	_____

_____
- -

1. The mother duck sits and _____ .

_____
- -

2. Now the last one _____ .

_____
- - - - - - - - - - - - - - - - - - - -

3. She _____ them what to do.

_____
- -

4. "Do not walk into _____ ."

Name _____

1	Nell and Bob were _____ - _____ together.	sliding sitting swimming
2	_____ - The bus _____ at Jim's house.	stopped said smiled
3	They saw Jim's dog _____ - _____ a rabbit.	chatting chasing shaving
4	_____ - They _____ the rabbit would get away.	hoped hopped hogged
5	_____ - The rabbit _____ into a hole.	hoped hopped hogged

Harcourt Brace School Publishers

Name _____

Circle and write the word that completes each sentence.

1	Dad _____ the cake.	moves washes mixes
2	Rose _____ from the window.	watches wants walks
3	Tom's _____ _____ come.	animals friends coaches
4	They put the _____ on a table.	bags boxes blocks
5	Then Tom _____ in. Surprise!	cares cakes comes
6	He will make two birthday _____.	wishes washes watches

Harcourt Brace School Publishers

Read the story. Then write words from the story to complete the sentences.

Tim and I climbed up the sagging steps and looked in the window. We saw boxes and dusty tables. We walked in. The creaking made us afraid. Tim felt a tapping on his head. Then a big blob chased us out of the house!

I screamed and woke up. Mom hugged me and tucked me in again. It was only a dream.

1. The house's steps were _____ .

2. A scary blob _____ the children.

3. The girl's mother _____

her and _____ her in.

Name _____

1	The animals _____ ---------------------------- _____ all day.	planted put played
2	Some of them _____ ---------------------------- _____ .	hoped hopped helped
3	And some of them _____ ---------------------------- _____ .	danced drilled dripped
4	Then they were _____ ---------------------------- _____ down.	sitting sliding stopping
5	This one just _____ ---------------------------- _____ them.	works was watches

Harcourt Brace School Publishers

Name _____

Fill in the circle next to the word that completes each sentence. Then write the word.

1	Rabbit _____ out of his hole.	○ hooted ○ helped ○ hopped
2	Pony was _____ the king's garden.	○ eating ○ sitting ○ washing
3	"Stop," said Rabbit, "or the _____ will not grow."	○ parts ○ places ○ plants
4	"This garden is _____ too fast!"	○ getting ○ growing ○ moving
5	"What if the king _____ you?"	○ closes ○ comes ○ catches
6	"Then he will be _____," said Pony.	○ sitting ○ surprised ○ shouted

Harcourt Brace School Publishers

Name _____

Add **ed** and **ing** to each word. You may need to add or drop letters.

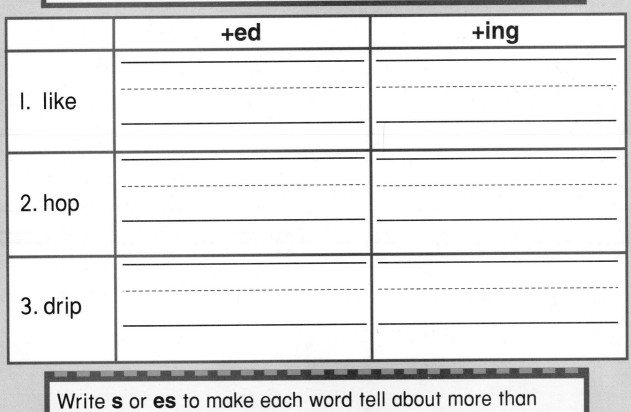

	+ed	+ing
1. like		
2. hop		
3. drip		

Write **s** or **es** to make each word tell about more than one. Then trace the whole word.

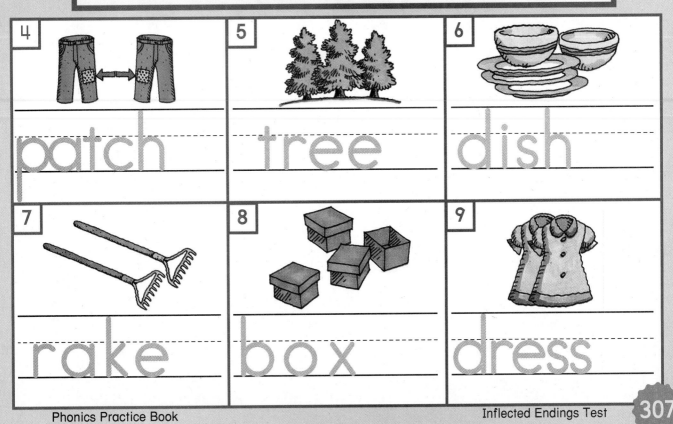

4. patch

5. tree

6. dish

7. rake

8. box

9. dress

Cut-Out Fold-Up Books

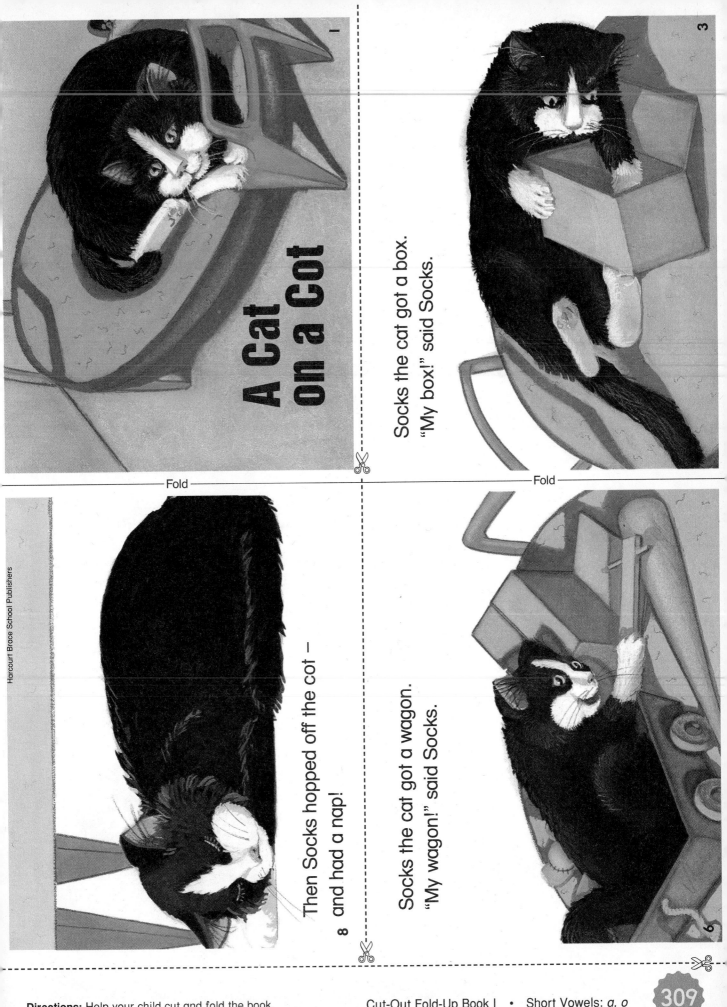

1

A Cat
on a Cot

3

Socks the cat got a box.
"My box!" said Socks.

Then Socks hopped off the cot —
8 and had a nap!

Socks the cat got a wagon.
"My wagon!" said Socks.

6

Harcourt Brace School Publishers

Directions: Help your child cut and fold the book.

Cut-Out Fold-Up Book I • Short Vowels: *a, o*

4

Socks the cat got a bat.
"My bat!" said Socks.

2

Socks the cat had a cot.
"My cot!" said Socks.

Harcourt Brace School Publishers

—Fold—

—Fold—

Socks the cat got a doll.
"My doll!" said Socks.

Socks sat on the cot with the box,
...the bat, the doll, and the wagon.

5

7

Cut-Out Fold-Up Book I • Short Vowels: a, o

Directions: Help your child cut and fold the book.

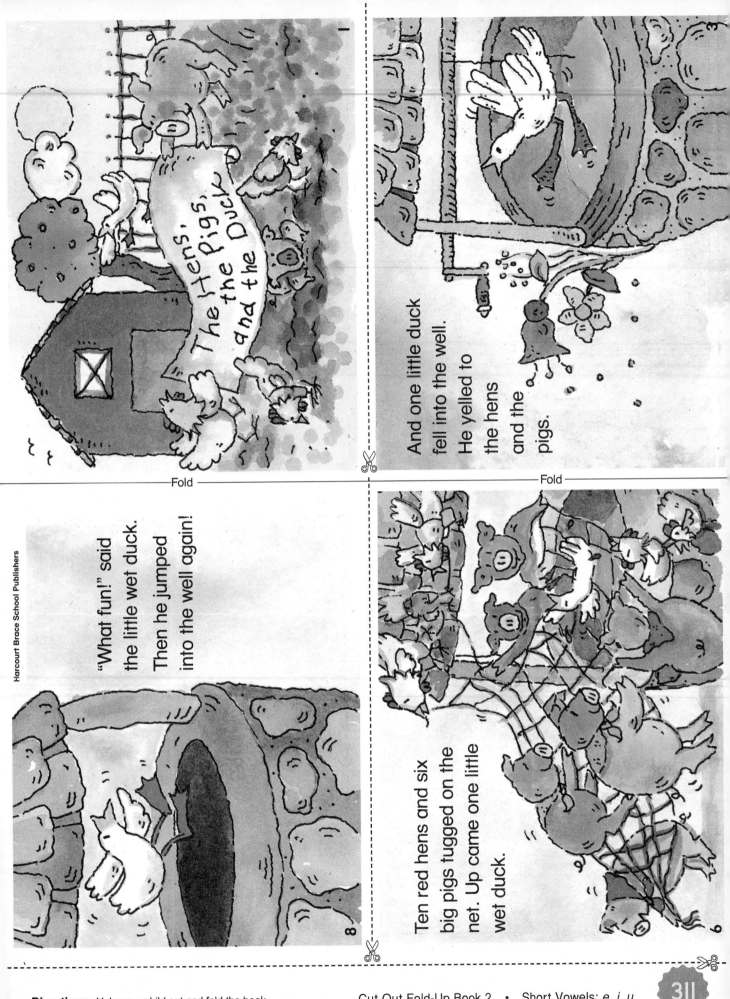

1

The Hens,
the Pigs,
and the Duck

3

And one little duck
fell into the well.
He yelled to
the hens
and the
pigs.

Harcourt Brace School Publishers

"What fun!" said
the little wet duck.
Then he jumped
into the well again!

8

Ten red hens and six
big pigs tugged on the
net. Up came one little
wet duck.

6

Directions: Help your child cut and fold the book.

Cut-Out Fold-Up Book 2 • Short Vowels: *e, i, u*

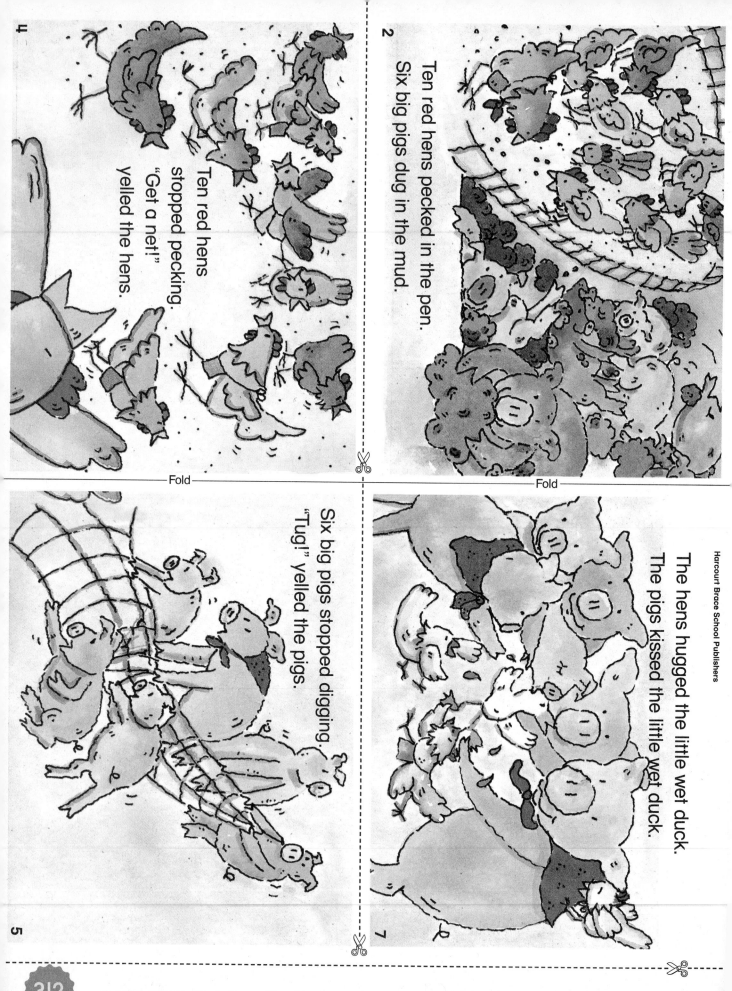

4

Ten red hens
stopped pecking.
"Get a net!"
yelled the hens.

2

Ten red hens pecked in the pen.
Six big pigs dug in the mud.

Fold

Fold

Six big pigs stopped digging.
"Tug!" yelled the pigs.

The hens hugged the little wet duck.
The pigs kissed the little wet duck.

Harcourt Brace School Publishers

5

7

Cut-Out Fold-Up Book 2 • Short Vowels: *e, i, u*

Directions: Help your child cut and fold the book.

Mike Mole's Home

One day, Rose Toad rode up on her bike. Rose poked her nose in Mike Mole's hole.

Fold

Fold

Mike Mole was having a fine time. To a mole, a home in a hole is just right!

One night, Bo Goat was in his boat in the cove. "Hi, Mike," yelled Bo. Come for a boat ride."

Harcourt Brace School Publishers

8

9

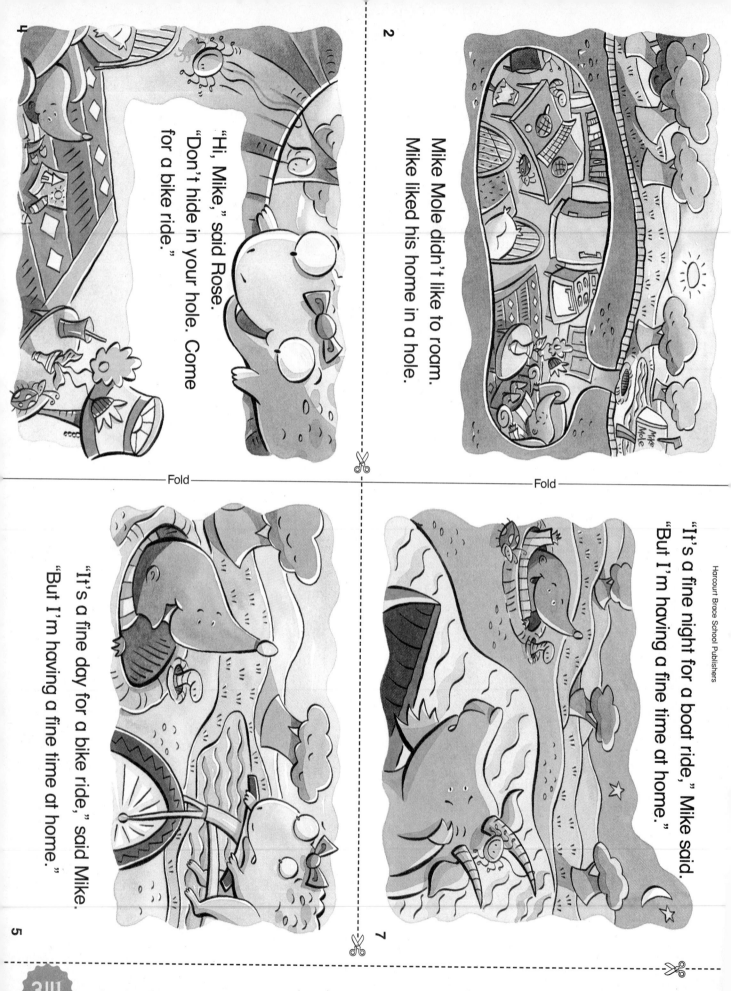

2
Mike Mole didn't like to roam.
Mike liked his home in a hole.

4
"Hi, Mike," said Rose.
"Don't hide in your hole. Come
for a bike ride."

Harcourt Brace School Publishers

7
"It's a fine night for a boat ride," Mike said.
"But I'm having a fine time at home."

5
"It's a fine day for a bike ride," said Mike.
"But I'm having a fine time at home."

Directions: Help your child cut and fold the book.

Jean and Jake

Jean waded into the lake. Jake played near her in the weeds.

3

The toad made a huge leap onto the beach. "We saved it, Jake," said Jean.

8

Jean peeked under a leaf. There was a little toad.

9

Directions: Help your child cut and fold the book.

Cut-Out Fold-Up Book 4 • Long Vowels: *e, a, u*

4

What did Jake see?
What could it be?

Fold

2

Jean and her
dog Jake went to
the lake one day.

Fold

5

"Stay by this tree," said Jean.
Jean could hear a "beep-peep."

7

Harcourt Brace School Publishers

Jean said, "Please Jake,
help me save this
cute toad."

Cut-Out Fold-Up Book 4 • Long Vowels: *e, a, u*

Directions: Help your child cut and fold the book.

The Quick Storm

1

The thunder claps and the breeze blows.
We open the tent flap to watch the storm.

3

Then all is still. The storm leaves as quickly as it came. Were you ever stuck in a storm?

8

A cold blast of wind blows in. We are a little scared. When will it stop?

9

Harcourt Brace School Publishers

Directions: Help your child cut and fold the book.   Cut-Out Fold-Up Book 5   •   Clusters and Digraphs

317

4

Then rain begins to drop on the tent. Drops start dripping into the tent.

2

Just as we are going to sleep, we see a bright flash of light.

Fold

Fold

5

Another flash, and the crack of a branch. That was close!

7

The rain slacks off, and the thunder stops coming so fast.

Harcourt Brace School Publishers

Cut-Out Fold-Up Book 5 • Clusters and Digraphs

Directions: Help your child cut and fold the book.

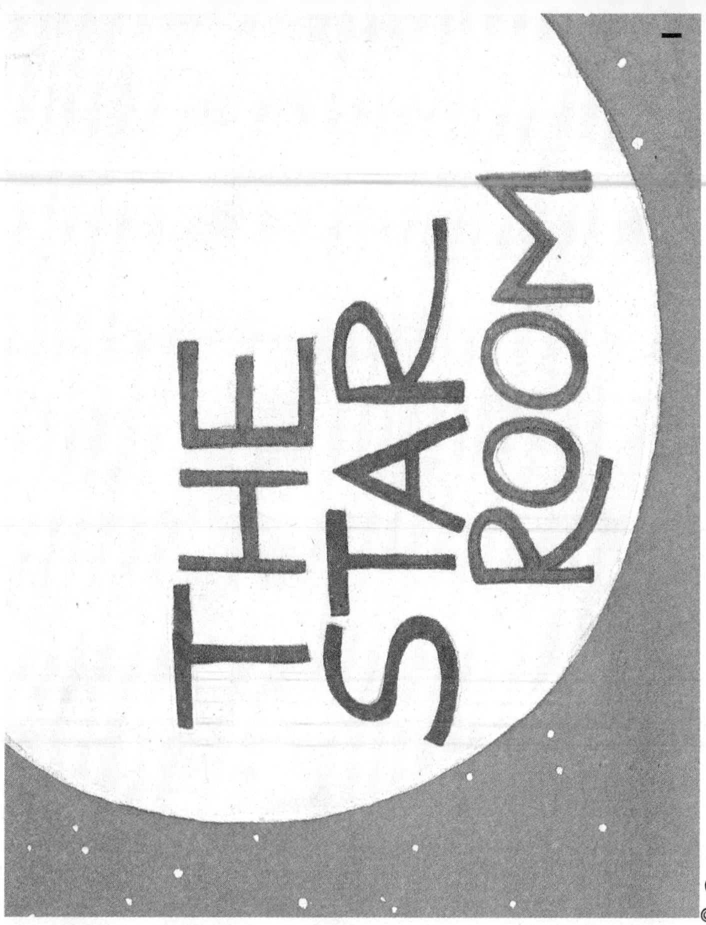

THE STAR ROOM

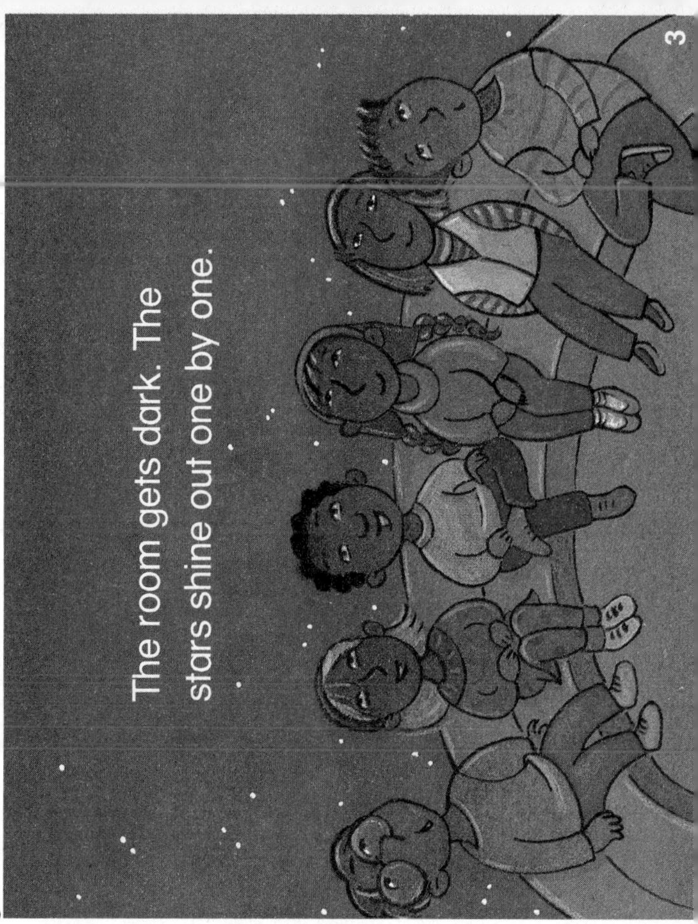

The room gets dark. The stars shine out one by one.

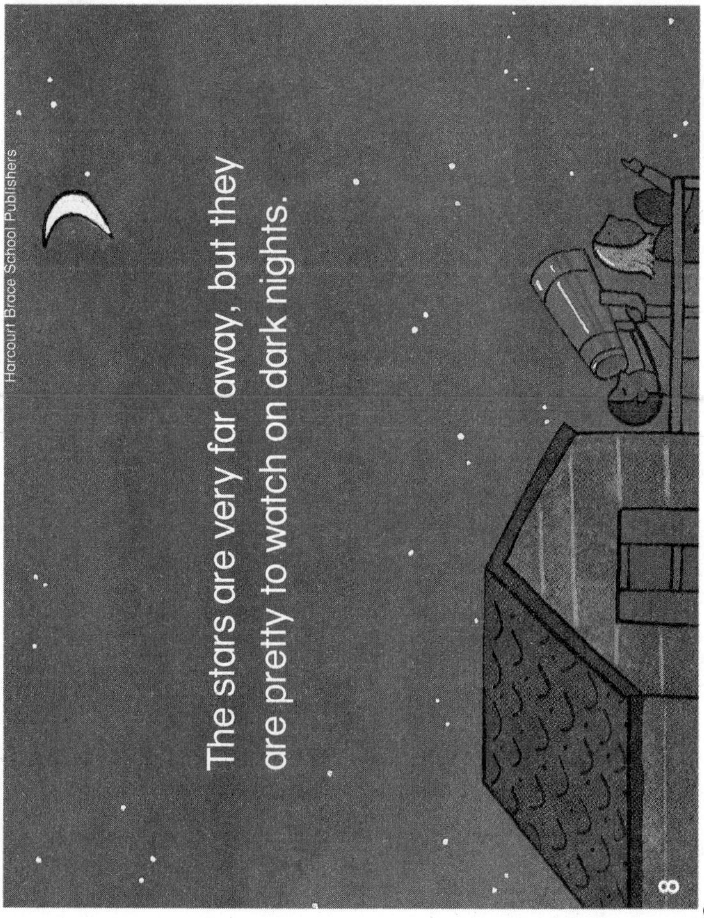

The stars are very far away, but they are pretty to watch on dark nights.

8

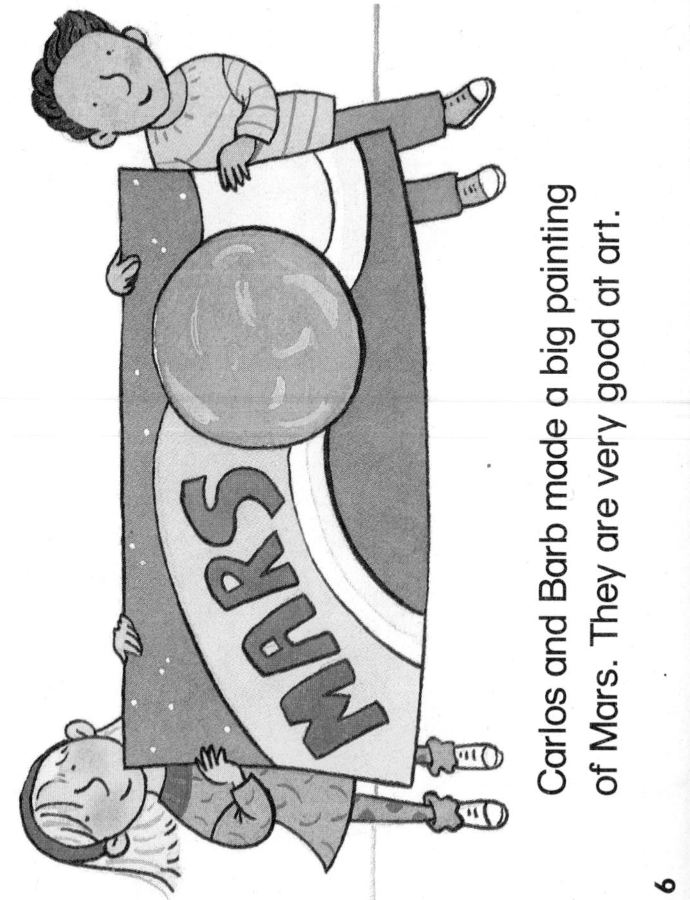

Carlos and Barb made a big painting of Mars. They are very good at art.

MARS

6

4

One day our class went there.
We saw what Mars looks like.

Fold

2

In one part of the park, there is a place to see stars.

Fold

When we got back, we had art. We made paintings of the stars.

5

Harcourt Brace School Publishers

Mark is smart. He reads a lot about stars and Mars.

7

PLANETARIUM

STARS

MARS

Cut-Out Fold-Up Book 6 • *R*-Controlled Vowel: / är / *ar*

Directions: Help your child cut and fold the book.